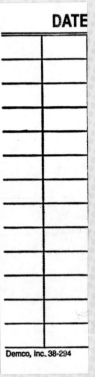

MICHAEL CHABON

PRESENTS

WRITER

BRIAN K. VAUGHAN

ARTISTS

STEVE ROLSTON
JASON SHAWN ALEXANDER
PHILIP BOND
EDUARDO BARRETO

COLORISTS

DAVE STEWART
MATTHEW HOLLINGSWORTH
PAUL HORNSCHEMEIER
DAN JACKSON

LETTERER

TOM ORZECHOWSKI

COVER ARTIST

ALEX ROSS

PRESTIDIGITATOR

MICHAEL CHABON

INSPIRED BY

The Amazing Adventures of Kavalier & Clay
by MICHAEL CHABON

DARK HORSE BOOKS®

INTRODUCTION

BY MICHAEL CHABON

ONE WEEKEND TOWARD the end of his public life, as he and his ex-wife plied their yearly course along the circuit of comic book conventions, bickering, bantering, holding each other up when the sidewalks were icy or the stairs steep, Sam Clay found himself in Cleveland, Ohio, as a guest of honor at the 1986 ErieCon. ErieCon was a mid-sized regional show held in the ballroom of a Euclid Avenue hotel that stood, until it was demolished, across the street from a grand old movie palace that soon after also succumbed to the wrecking ball, during one of the spasms of redevelopment that have tormented Cleveland's slumber for the past forty years.

> *"I'm an escape artist,"*
> *the boy said at last,*
> *making it sound dull,*
> *offhand, disappointing,*
> *the way he might*
> *have said, "I have*
> *a shellfish allergy."*

People who saw them making the con scene in those years were often touched by the steadfast way that Rosa Kavalier—born Rosa Luxemburg Saks in New York City in 1919 and known to the world, if at all, as Rose Saxon, a queen of the romance comics—kept hold of the elbow of one of her ex-husband's trademark loud blazers as they moved from curb to counter, from ballroom to elevator, from bar to dining room. They were, people said, devoted to each other. And undoubtedly this was the case. They had known each other for more than forty-five years, and though no one ever quite untangled the complicated narrative of their various creative and romantic partnerships over the years, mutual devotion was certainly part of the story. But the truth of the tight grip that Rosa kept on Sam was that, after a series of unsuccessful operations to repair his damaged retinas, the man could barely see a foot in front of his face.

"She's my seeing-eye dog," he would say, and then he would wait, wearing a short-sighted grin, as if daring his ex-wife to find no humor in his witticism, a challenge she was always ready to accept.

But to the people who knew Sam—old-timers, friends, and enemies from the Golden and Silver Ages, the beaming young (or formerly young) protégés who regularly radiated from the formless warmth of the Kavalier-Clay ménage—it was obvious how humiliating he found his poor vision, his lousy teeth, the hobbled, foot-dragging gait that had resulted from the surprise return, when he hit his sixties, of the polio that crippled him as a boy. Sam Clay was a professionally (if not always convincingly) fierce man whose mighty shoulders and Popeye forearms attested to a lifelong regimen of pushups, dumbbells, and the punching of speed bags. You could see that he hated every moment he had to spend "hanging around Rosa," in his own formulation, "like a persistent fart."

On this particular Saturday afternoon in Cleveland, Ohio, in 1986, therefore, when it came time for Sam to transfer custody, from his plumbing system to the hotel's, of the Dr. Pepper-and-orange-juice cocktail (mixed by a secret formula known and palatable only to him) that he been swilling from a thermos all morning, Sam got up from the "Kavalier & Clay" table in Artists' Alley and set forth alone to find the men's room, which, according to the guy at the next table, lay just a few steps outside and to the left of the Cuyahoga Ballroom's gilded doors. How hard could it be? Rosa was off somewhere having a confab with some skinny little thing named Diana from Comico, and Sam's new assistant Mark Morgenstern (later known for his work on the DC/Vertigo revival of the old Pharaoh Comics title *Earthman*) was attending the Klaus Nordling tribute panel. And Sammy, Sam decided, could goddamn well find his own goddamn way to the toilet.

As it turned out, there was no bathroom just outside and to the left of the ballroom's gilded doors; or perhaps the ballroom had more doors than Sam knew about, or featured less

gilding than he had been led to expect; or maybe, he thought bitterly, he was just so addled-pated and purblind that he no longer knew his left from his right. He spent ten minutes blundering around the elevator lobby, responding with cheerful irritation to greetings and good wishes from blurred faces and voices that sounded as though he ought to know them. But his attention was wholly occupied with the effort it cost him not to appear to be lost, blind, and in desperate need of a pee, so that he might as well have been in a crowd of strangers. There was an unpleasant incident with a large potted fern and a compromising entanglement with the legs of a display easel. Sam's dignity—an attribute with which, until quite recently, he had never been unduly burdened—would not, it appeared, permit him to admit that he was in need of assistance.

At one point he found himself in an intimate, metallic space whose acoustics suggested a washroom or stall, and he knew a horrible instant of hope and relief before realizing that he was in fact riding an elevator. He got off at some floor and walked in some direction, trailing his right hand against the dark-red softness of the hallway's flocked wallpaper because once, many years before, in an issue of *Astounding*, he had read that you could always count on finding your way in and out of any labyrinth as long as, from the moment you entered it, you kept one hand in continuous contact with one wall. This expedient may, or may not, have had something to do with the fact that, twenty-five minutes after setting out from Artists' Alley full of piss and confidence, he succeeded, not without effort, in locking himself inside a broom closet.

Like most grave mistakes, his became apparent more or less upon commission. The bright, burgundy, flocked-velvet blur of the hallway went black. The door shut behind him with the decisive click of some instrument of execution snapping to. There was an acrid bubblegum stink of disinfectant and the damp-bedsheet smell of old mop heads. Sammy knew a moment of pure infantile dread. Then in the darkness he smiled.

"At least," he pointed out to himself, unzipping his fly, "there'll be a bucket."

With a chiming like some liquid carillon he relieved himself into the rolling mop bucket whose contours his shoetips then fingertips had revealed to him. Bliss, fulfillment through evacuation. He zipped up and began, with fresh dread, to contemplate the impossible task that lay before him, which consisted of shouldering the now almost unendurable and infinitely imperiled burden of his dignity while pounding on the door of the broom closet and screaming for help until he was hoarse, all the while enjoying the piscine bouquet of his own urine. He opened his mouth, ready to scream. Then he closed his mouth, experiencing second thoughts about this course. When, after all, they finally discovered his corpse, or perhaps his skeleton, in this closet, huddled over a bucket of ancient pee, that would perhaps be embarrassing for *some* people—but not for him, because he would be dead. He slapped the door once, twice with the flat of his hand. He leaned against a steel shelf stacked with rolls of toilet paper in their paper wrappers, and readied himself for the final indignity, and sighed.

There was a rattle—the doorknob—and then an insect scratching, wire feelers. And then a burst of light and air.

"I saw you go in," said a boy. "Then I heard knocking." A boy in a red baseball cap. An open mouth, maybe some kind of dirt around the mouth. Sammy leaned forward to get a better look. About ten years old, a standard-issue little American kid but with something sly in his eyes and an overall air of injury or grievance. He was wearing a red jersey with the word LIONS running in old-timey script across the front, and in his hand he held an open Swiss army knife. The grime on his lips a streak of chocolate, a chocolate crumb or two. A Hostess cupcake, or perhaps a Ding Dong.

"It smells kind of like pee in there," the boy said.

"God, you're right!" said Sam, waving his hand back and forth in front of his face. "This hotel really is a dump."

He stepped out of the closet and shut the door behind him.

"Hey, thanks, kid. Guess I—" But what was the point of lying? Would he ever see this kid again? *Guess I just wandered into a closet.* "Guess I had the wrong room. Thanks." He and the boy shook hands, the boy's boneless and reluctant in his. He gestured with his chin to the little red knife. "Pretty handy with that. What are you, the world's youngest second-story man? Hotel dick know about you?"

The boy blinked, as if doubting his own reply or the wisdom of even making it. His breathing came wheezy through congested nostrils.

"I'm an escape artist," the boy said at last, making it sound dull, offhand, disappointing, the way he might have said, "I have a shellfish allergy."

"That so?" Sam felt his heart squeeze at the sound of the words *escape artist*, the deviated-septum rasp, the eyes that sought to slip free of the enforced deadpan manner of a ten-year-old boy. "Good with locks?"

The kid shrugged.

"Yours was easy." The boy refolded the pick blade into his knife and returned it to the pocket of his jeans. "I'm actually not really all that good."

In his semi-blindness it took a moment for Sam to realize that the boy was crying, softly, and had been crying possibly for a long time before he took it upon himself to rescue the old guy in the closet.

"Hmm," he said. "So what are you doing, wandering around the hotel, freeing strange geezers from broom closets? Where are your mother and father?"

The kid shrugged.

"I'm supposed to be downstairs. At the league award lunch."

"You like baseball?"

Another shrug.

"I take it they aren't handing you any awards."

The boy reached into the pocket of his blue jeans again and took out a crumpled wad of paper. He handed it wordlessly to Sammy with an expression on his face of utter disdain for the paper and its contents. Sammy unfolded and smoothed it out and then pressed it right up to his right eye, the stronger, to read it.

"'Nice Try Citation,'" he said.

The boy leaned back against the far wall of the corridor and sank slowly to the ground until his forehead touched his knees.

"Long season?" Sammy said, after a moment.

"Ninth place," the boy said, his voice muffled and small. "Out of nine. Also I have personal problems I don't care to discuss."

Sam considered pressing, but decided that when you were ten, all your problems were more or less personal.

"Look at me," Sam said. "I just peed into a bucket."

This seemed to make the boy feel better about himself.

"Listen. I don't know what the trouble is. I'm going to, uh, respect your privacy there. But I appreciate your helping me. I'd like to pay you back." He reached into the hip pocket of his suit pants and then remembered that his wallet was in the breast pocket of his jacket, hanging over the back of the chair in Artists' Alley. "Only I'm, uh, busted." He rubbed at the stubble on his chin. "So I guess I need to find somebody else who's stuck in a jam and do the same for them like you did for me. Creed of the League of the Golden Key."

"Huh?"

"Forget about it. What's your name?"

"Hey, dickhead!" A gang of boys, wearing red Lions jerseys and red caps tumbled into the hallway from the elevator and stood. "Vaughan!" The voice, cracking with mockery or pubescence, seemed to be issuing from the largest among them. "What the hell are you doing up here? Coach is looking everywhere for you! He called your *mommy*, dickhead!"

"You best get your ass downstairs!"

"Hey, Vaughan, who's the old guy?"

Sammy took a step toward the boy, Vaughan, and lowered his voice.

"They want to give you another certificate?"

"A trophy. But I saw mine. The head was missing. I guess maybe somebody, well. Broke it off. When I saw that, that's when I left."

"Come *on*, Vaughan!"

"Hey," Sam told the boys, flexing his Popeye arms, and putting as much Brooklyn into his voice as he could muster. It was, still, a decent amount. "Whyn't you punks get the hell out of here and leave the kid alone?"

The red mass hung a moment in the hallway, wavering like the afterimage of a bright flash on his damaged retinas. Then a moment later it was gone.

"You ever read comic books?" Sam asked the boy.

"Not really. Like, Archies?"

"Archies. No, well, Archie has his place. But—"

Sam reached a hand down and offered to help the boy to his feet.

"Look, they got a big show going on downstairs. Cuyahoga Ballroom. A comics show. You might like it. Take Doctor Strange. He's a magician. You'd like that one, I bet."

"I've heard of him."

"You ought to check it out."

He pulled the boy up and stepped away from him.

"I'd better get back to the banquet," the boy said.

"Suit yourself," Sam said. "'Suit yourself,' that's good advice. I wish somebody'd given it to me when I was your age."

They went to the elevator and the boy pressed the button. They said nothing when it arrived and the doors opened, and nothing until they were halfway down.

"'Suit yourself,'" the boy repeated. "I let you out of a dark, stinky closet where you could've died; you give me some cheap advice."

Sam looked at the boy and saw that sly light in the boy's eyes again.

"Ten-year-olds," Sam said, as he got out of the elevator at the mezzanine. "God help me." The doors started to close on the boy and his chance to redeem himself and repay his debt of freedom. He stuck his arm in and stopped them from closing. "Check out the show," he said. "*That's* my advice to you. Cheap as it may be."

"I can't," the boy said. "I really don't think I can. But, uh, thanks."

"Vaughan. What's the rest of it?"

"Brian K. Vaughan." It came out in a rush, a single word, almost a single syllable.

"Uh-huh. What's the K for?"

"Kellar."

"Like the magician. Self-decapitation, right? Harry Kellar. That the guy?"

Brian K. Vaughan looked shocked, almost put out, as if his middle initial represented a grave and powerful mystery of which he had hitherto believed himself the sole initiate.

"Yeah," he said wonderingly.

Sam stepped back from the doors, and drew back his hand with a Harry Kellar flourish, and the door slid shut on Brian K. Vaughan who, having called home from a pay phone in the lobby, received permission to stay after the league banquet and attend the remainder of the Saturday session of ErieCon '86, at which he purchased a copy of *Strange Tales* number 146 (featuring Baron Mordo, Dormammu, *and* the Ancient One), in Very Good condition, thus altering the entire course of his future life, not to mention the lives of those of us who are fortunate enough to know and appreciate the comic book genius so wildly and thoroughly on display (along with the estimable talents of Steve Rolston, Jason Alexander, Philip Bond, and Eduardo Barreto) in the pages that follow.

He and Sam Clay never saw or spoke to each other again. ⚬—

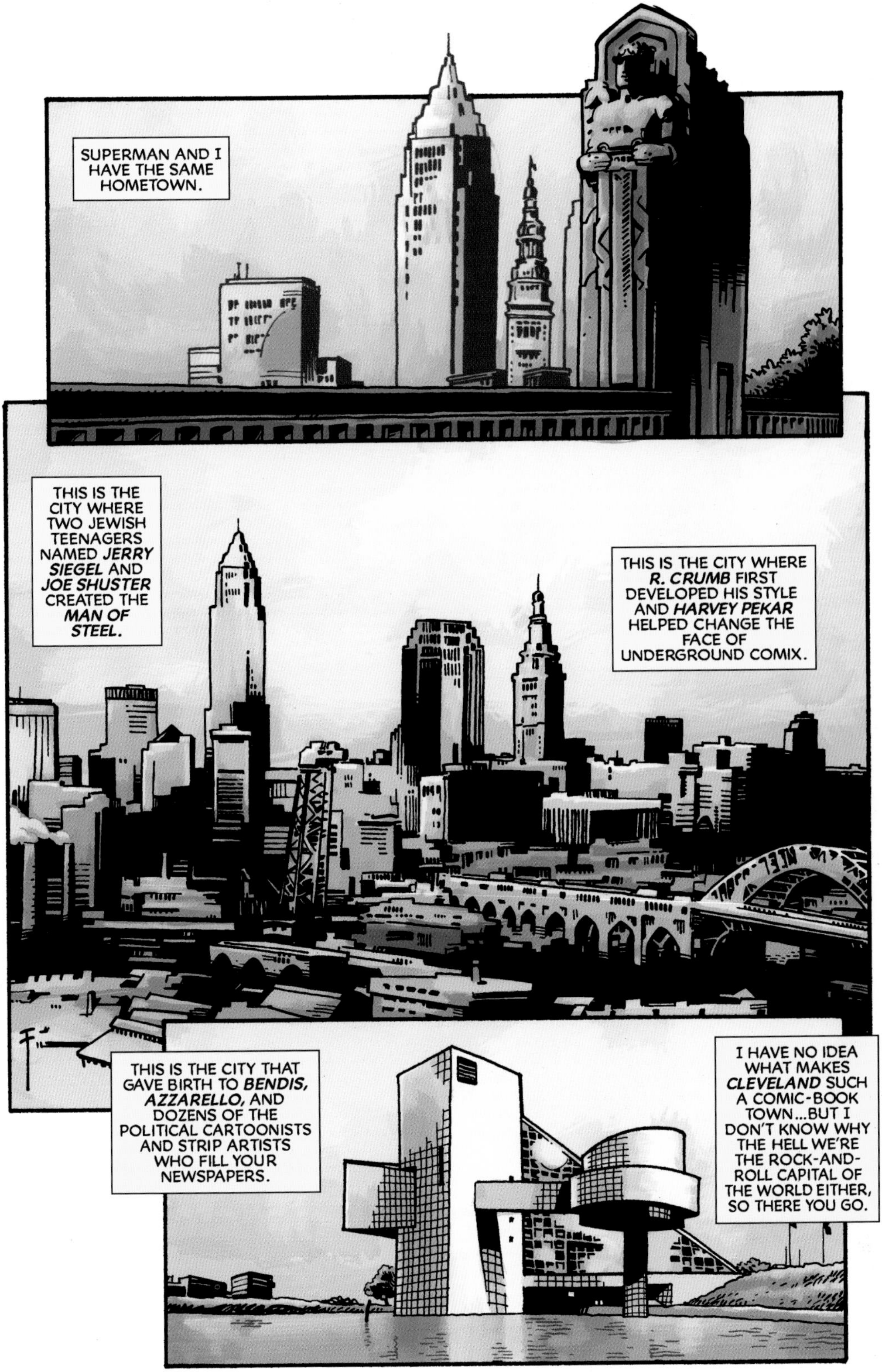
SUPERMAN AND I HAVE THE SAME HOMETOWN.
THIS IS THE CITY WHERE TWO JEWISH TEENAGERS NAMED *JERRY SIEGEL* AND *JOE SHUSTER* CREATED THE *MAN OF STEEL.*
THIS IS THE CITY WHERE *R. CRUMB* FIRST DEVELOPED HIS STYLE AND *HARVEY PEKAR* HELPED CHANGE THE FACE OF UNDERGROUND COMIX.
THIS IS THE CITY THAT GAVE BIRTH TO *BENDIS, AZZARELLO,* AND DOZENS OF THE POLITICAL CARTOONISTS AND STRIP ARTISTS WHO FILL YOUR NEWSPAPERS.
I HAVE NO IDEA WHAT MAKES *CLEVELAND* SUCH A COMIC-BOOK TOWN...BUT I DON'T KNOW WHY THE HELL WE'RE THE ROCK-AND-ROLL CAPITAL OF THE WORLD EITHER, SO THERE YOU GO.

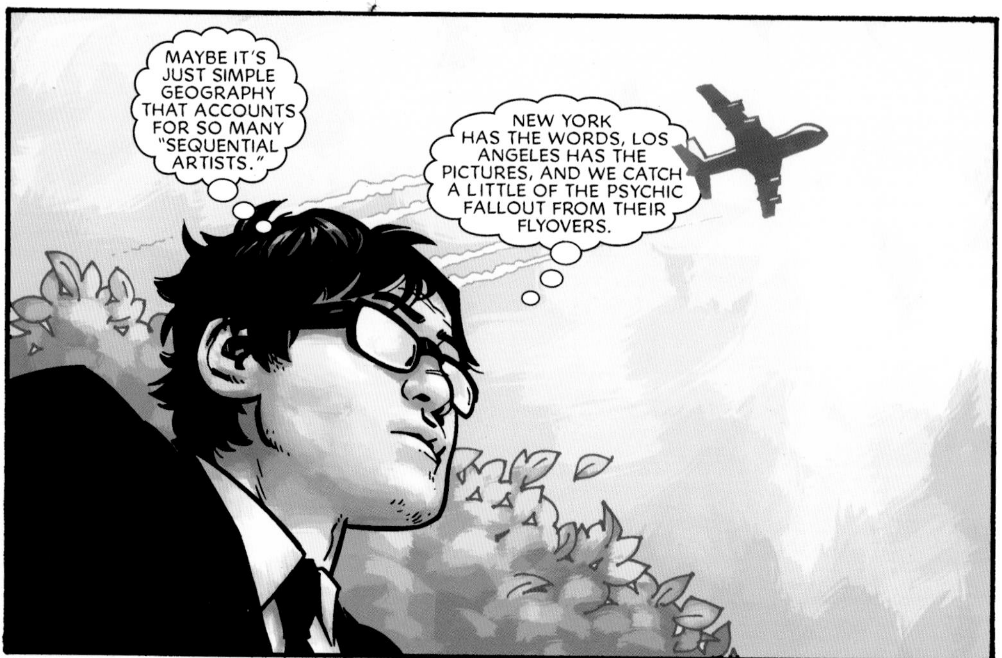
MAYBE IT'S JUST SIMPLE GEOGRAPHY THAT ACCOUNTS FOR SO MANY "SEQUENTIAL ARTISTS."
NEW YORK HAS THE WORDS, LOS ANGELES HAS THE PICTURES, AND WE CATCH A LITTLE OF THE PSYCHIC FALLOUT FROM THEIR FLYOVERS.

OR MAYBE IT'S SOMETHING IN THE WATER...

...NEW CHEMICAL COMPOUNDS PRODUCED IN LAKE ERIE, LIKE THE MAGICAL SERUMS THAT TURNED SO MANY MERE MORTALS OF FICTION INTO GOLDEN AGE DEMIGODS.

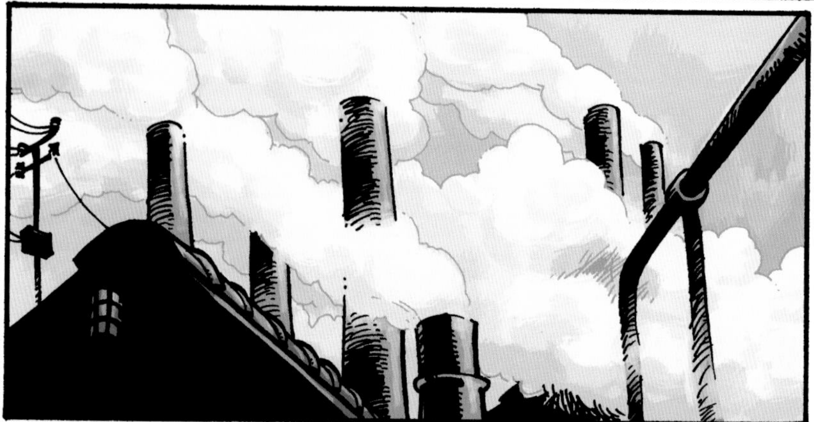

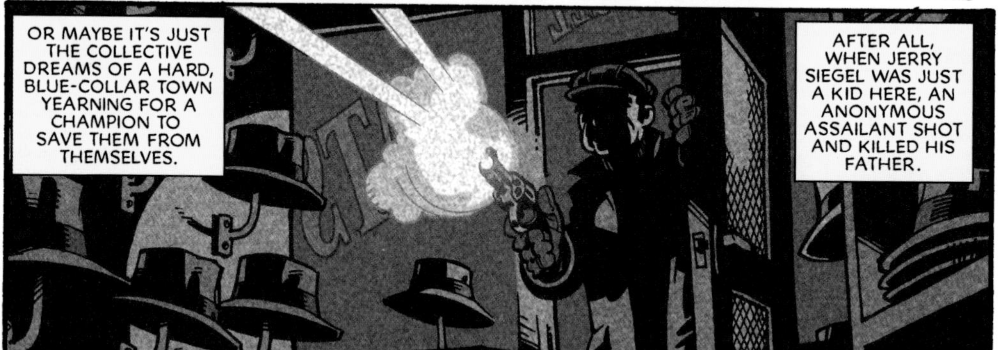
OR MAYBE IT'S JUST THE COLLECTIVE DREAMS OF A HARD, BLUE-COLLAR TOWN YEARNING FOR A CHAMPION TO SAVE THEM FROM THEMSELVES.
AFTER ALL, WHEN JERRY SIEGEL WAS JUST A KID HERE, AN ANONYMOUS ASSAILANT SHOT AND KILLED HIS FATHER.

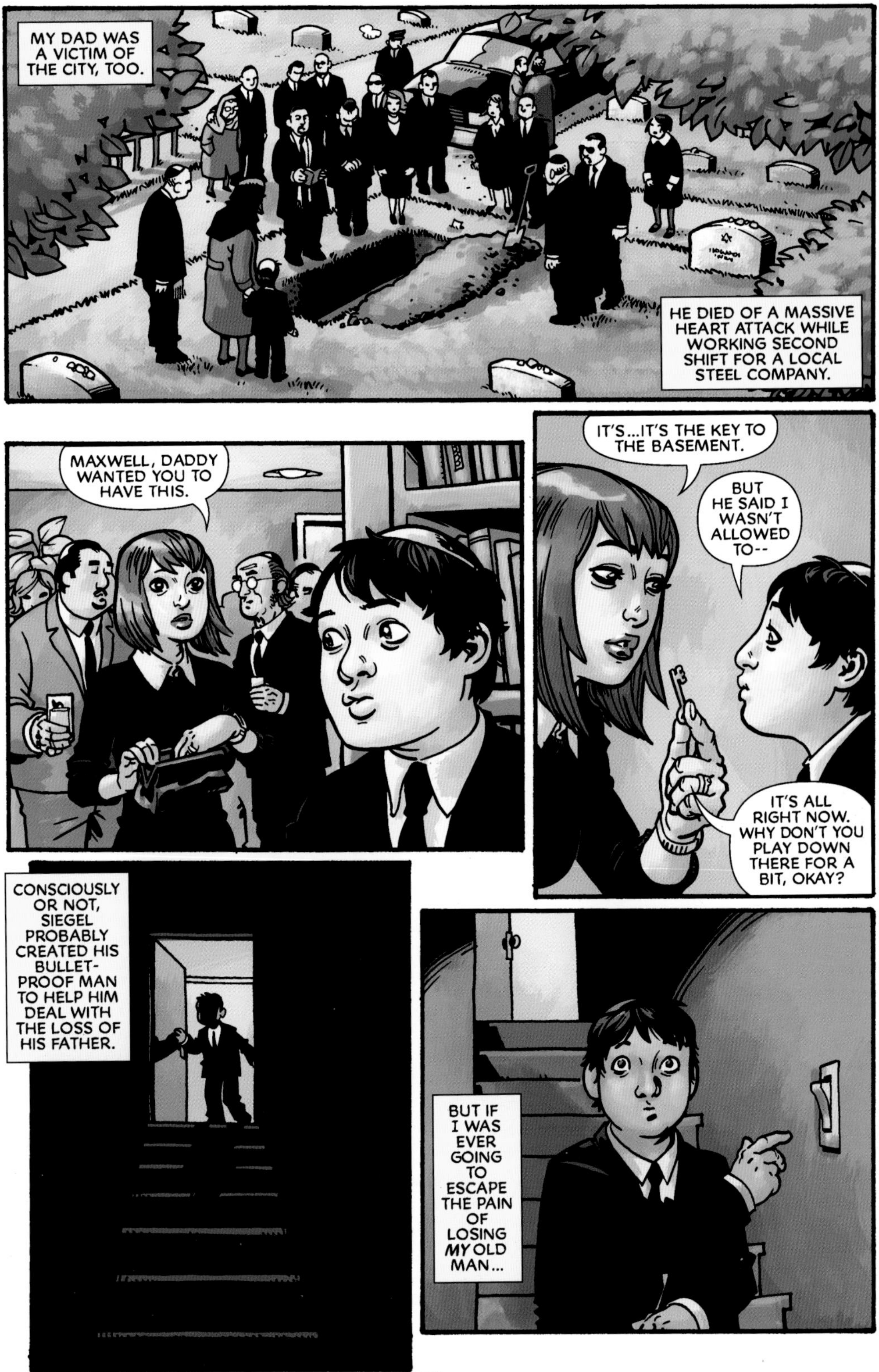
MY DAD WAS A VICTIM OF THE CITY, TOO.
HE DIED OF A MASSIVE HEART ATTACK WHILE WORKING SECOND SHIFT FOR A LOCAL STEEL COMPANY.
MAXWELL, DADDY WANTED YOU TO HAVE THIS.
IT'S...IT'S THE KEY TO THE BASEMENT.
BUT HE SAID I WASN'T ALLOWED TO--
IT'S ALL RIGHT NOW. WHY DON'T YOU PLAY DOWN THERE FOR A BIT, OKAY?
CONSCIOUSLY OR NOT, SIEGEL PROBABLY CREATED HIS BULLET-PROOF MAN TO HELP HIM DEAL WITH THE LOSS OF HIS FATHER.
BUT IF I WAS EVER GOING TO ESCAPE THE PAIN OF LOSING *MY* OLD MAN...

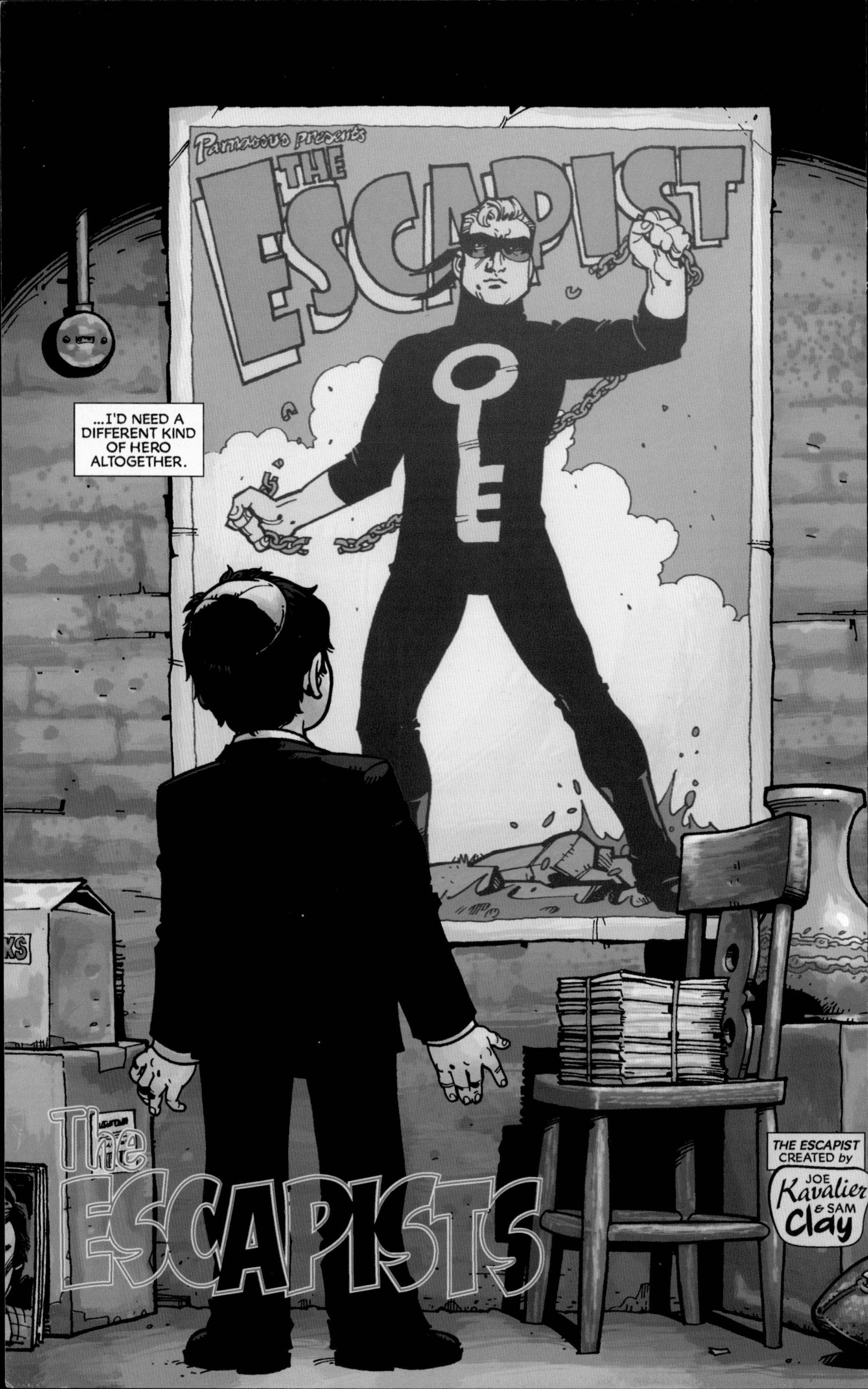

...I'D NEED A DIFFERENT KIND OF HERO ALTOGETHER.
Parnassus presents
THE ESCAPIST
The ESCAPISTS
THE ESCAPIST CREATED by JOE Kavalier & SAM Clay

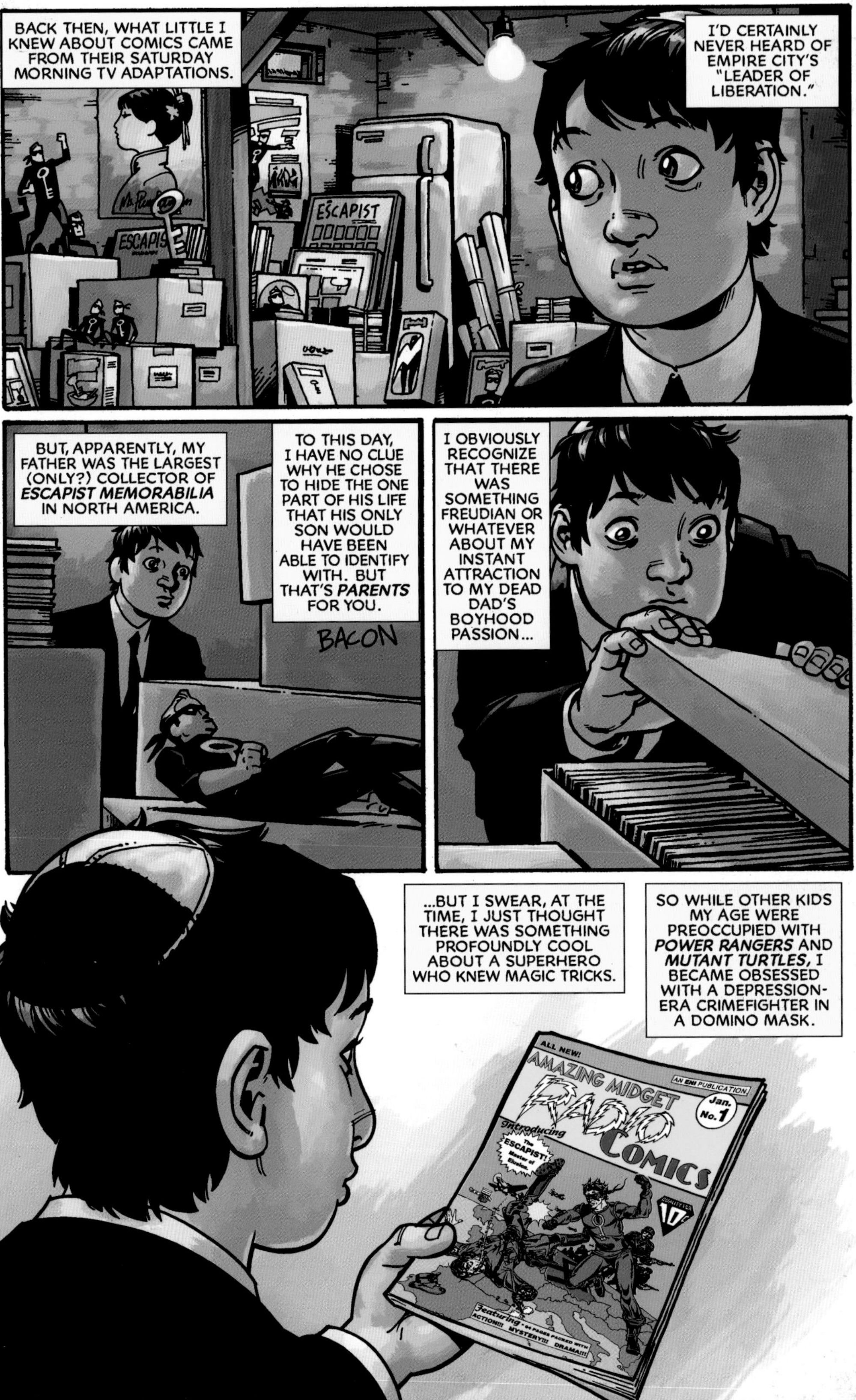
BACK THEN, WHAT LITTLE I KNEW ABOUT COMICS CAME FROM THEIR SATURDAY MORNING TV ADAPTATIONS.
I'D CERTAINLY NEVER HEARD OF EMPIRE CITY'S "LEADER OF LIBERATION."
ESCAPIST
ESCAPIST
BUT, APPARENTLY, MY FATHER WAS THE LARGEST (ONLY?) COLLECTOR OF *ESCAPIST MEMORABILIA* IN NORTH AMERICA.
TO THIS DAY, I HAVE NO CLUE WHY HE CHOSE TO HIDE THE ONE PART OF HIS LIFE THAT HIS ONLY SON WOULD HAVE BEEN ABLE TO IDENTIFY WITH. BUT THAT'S *PARENTS* FOR YOU.
BACON
I OBVIOUSLY RECOGNIZE THAT THERE WAS SOMETHING FREUDIAN OR WHATEVER ABOUT MY INSTANT ATTRACTION TO MY DEAD DAD'S BOYHOOD PASSION...
...BUT I SWEAR, AT THE TIME, I JUST THOUGHT THERE WAS SOMETHING PROFOUNDLY COOL ABOUT A SUPERHERO WHO KNEW MAGIC TRICKS.
SO WHILE OTHER KIDS MY AGE WERE PREOCCUPIED WITH *POWER RANGERS* AND *MUTANT TURTLES,* I BECAME OBSESSED WITH A DEPRESSION-ERA CRIMEFIGHTER IN A DOMINO MASK.
ALL NEW!
AMAZING MIDGET RADIO COMICS
Jan. No. 1
Introducing The ESCAPIST!

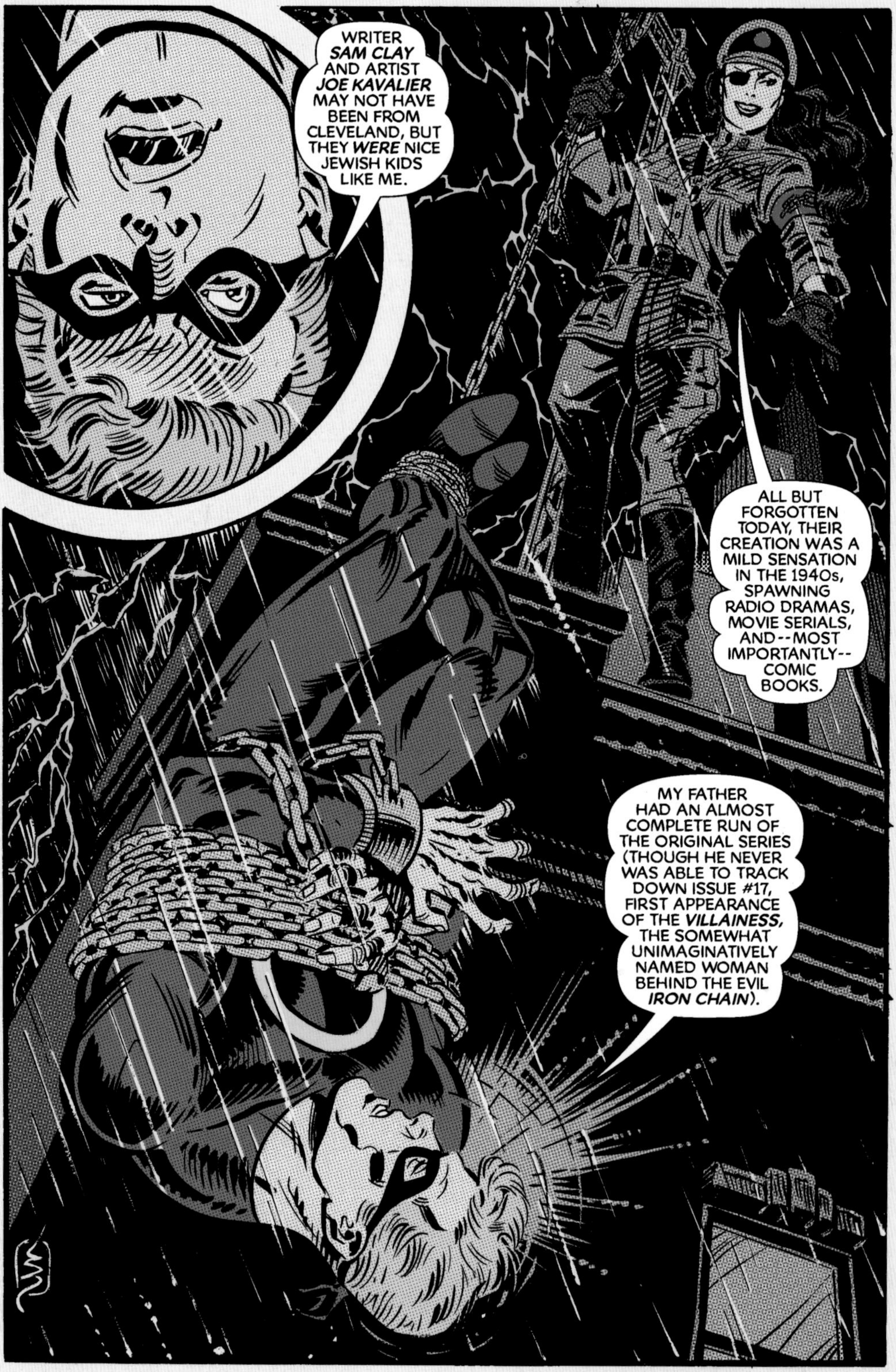
WRITER SAM CLAY AND ARTIST JOE KAVALIER MAY NOT HAVE BEEN FROM CLEVELAND, BUT THEY WERE NICE JEWISH KIDS LIKE ME.
ALL BUT FORGOTTEN TODAY, THEIR CREATION WAS A MILD SENSATION IN THE 1940s, SPAWNING RADIO DRAMAS, MOVIE SERIALS, AND--MOST IMPORTANTLY--COMIC BOOKS.
MY FATHER HAD AN ALMOST COMPLETE RUN OF THE ORIGINAL SERIES (THOUGH HE NEVER WAS ABLE TO TRACK DOWN ISSUE #17, FIRST APPEARANCE OF THE VILLAINESS, THE SOMEWHAT UNIMAGINATIVELY NAMED WOMAN BEHIND THE EVIL IRON CHAIN).

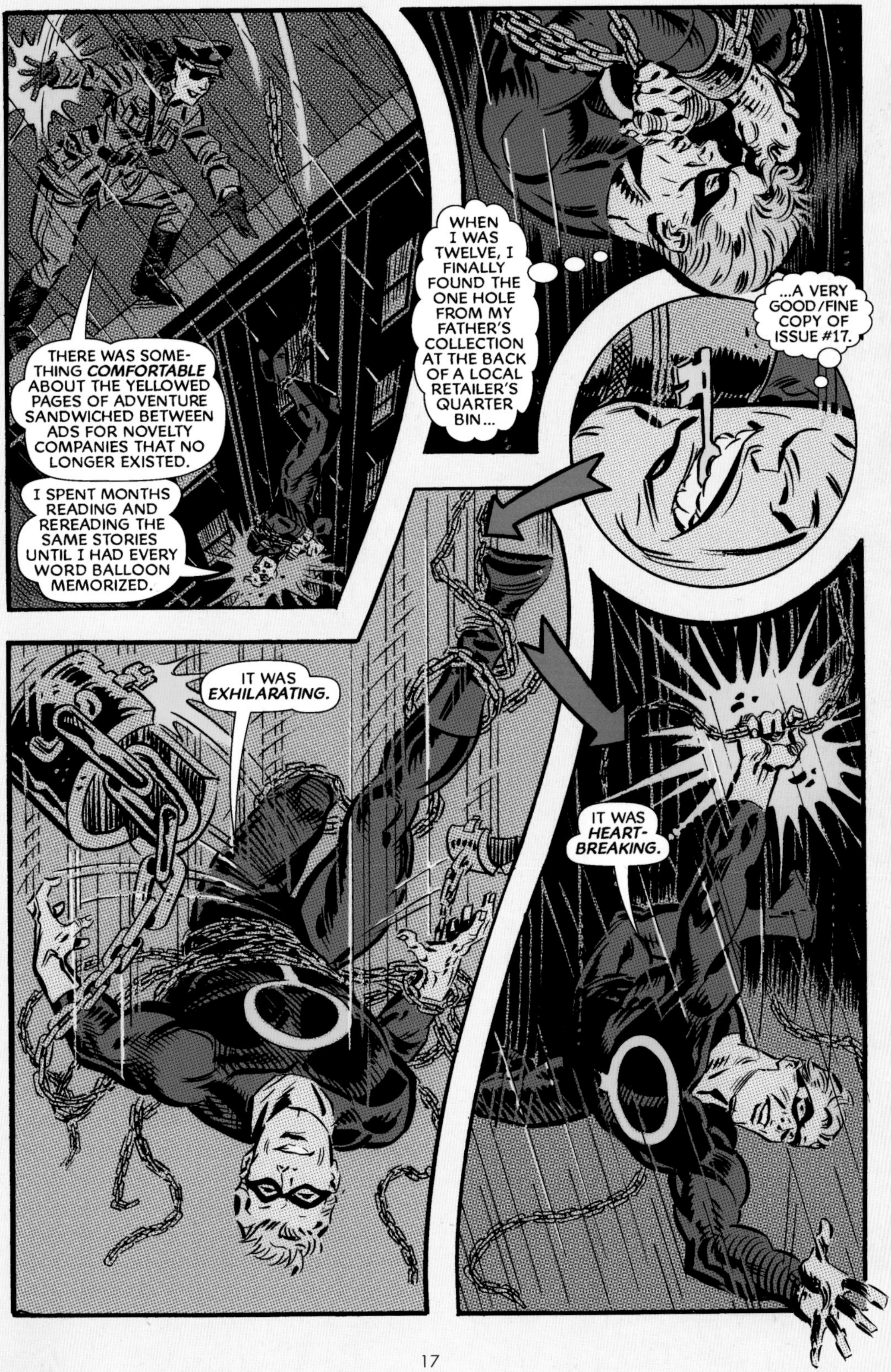
THERE WAS SOMETHING COMFORTABLE ABOUT THE YELLOWED PAGES OF ADVENTURE SANDWICHED BETWEEN ADS FOR NOVELTY COMPANIES THAT NO LONGER EXISTED.
I SPENT MONTHS READING AND REREADING THE SAME STORIES UNTIL I HAD EVERY WORD BALLOON MEMORIZED.
WHEN I WAS TWELVE, I FINALLY FOUND THE ONE HOLE FROM MY FATHER'S COLLECTION AT THE BACK OF A LOCAL RETAILER'S QUARTER BIN...
...A VERY GOOD/FINE COPY OF ISSUE #17.
IT WAS EXHILARATING.
IT WAS HEART-BREAKING.

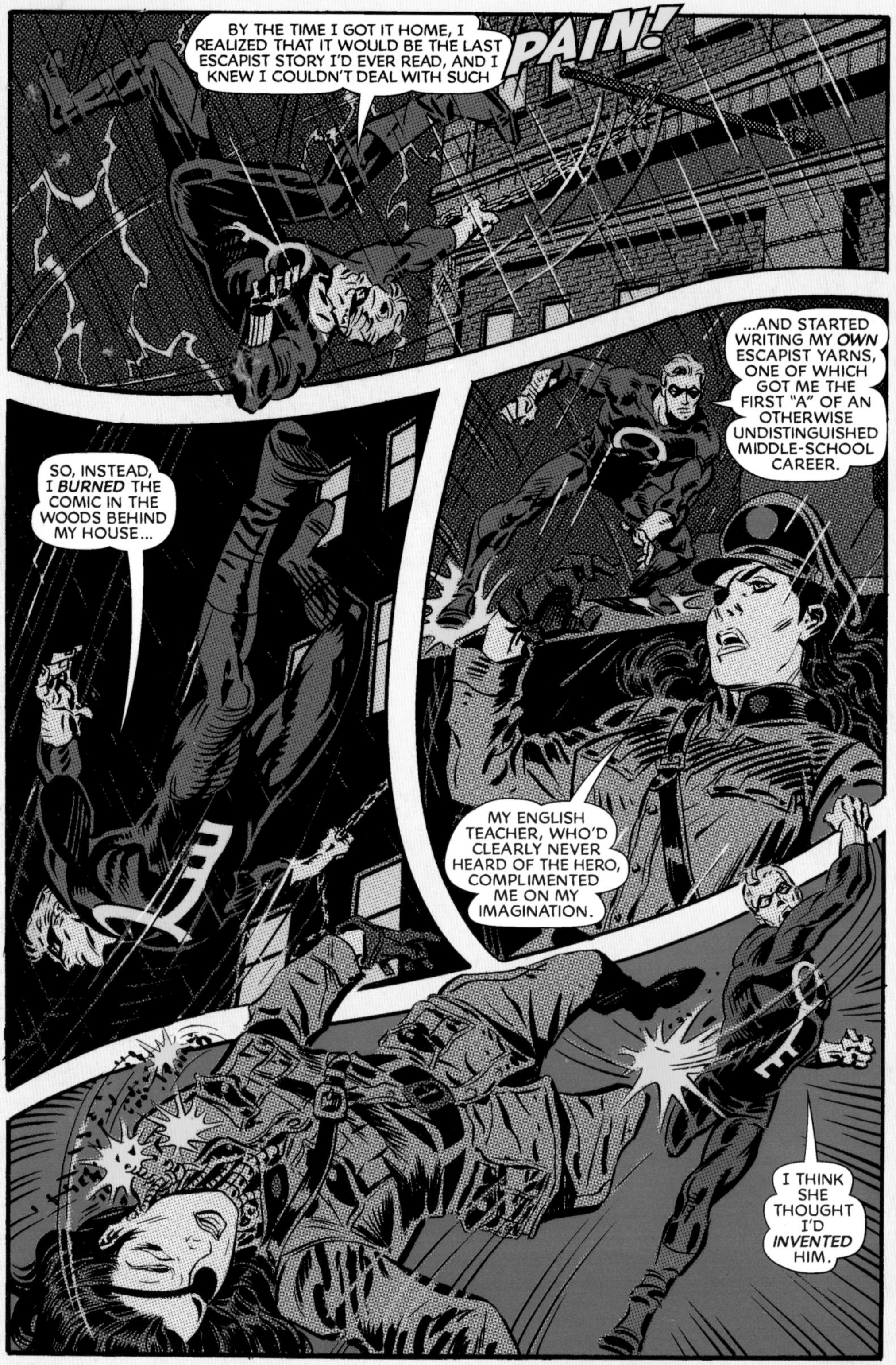
BY THE TIME I GOT IT HOME, I REALIZED THAT IT WOULD BE THE LAST ESCAPIST STORY I'D EVER READ, AND I KNEW I COULDN'T DEAL WITH SUCH
PAIN!
SO, INSTEAD, I *BURNED* THE COMIC IN THE WOODS BEHIND MY HOUSE...
...AND STARTED WRITING MY *OWN* ESCAPIST YARNS, ONE OF WHICH GOT ME THE FIRST "A" OF AN OTHERWISE UNDISTINGUISHED MIDDLE-SCHOOL CAREER.
MY ENGLISH TEACHER, WHO'D CLEARLY NEVER HEARD OF THE HERO, COMPLIMENTED ME ON MY IMAGINATION.
I THINK SHE THOUGHT I'D *INVENTED* HIM.

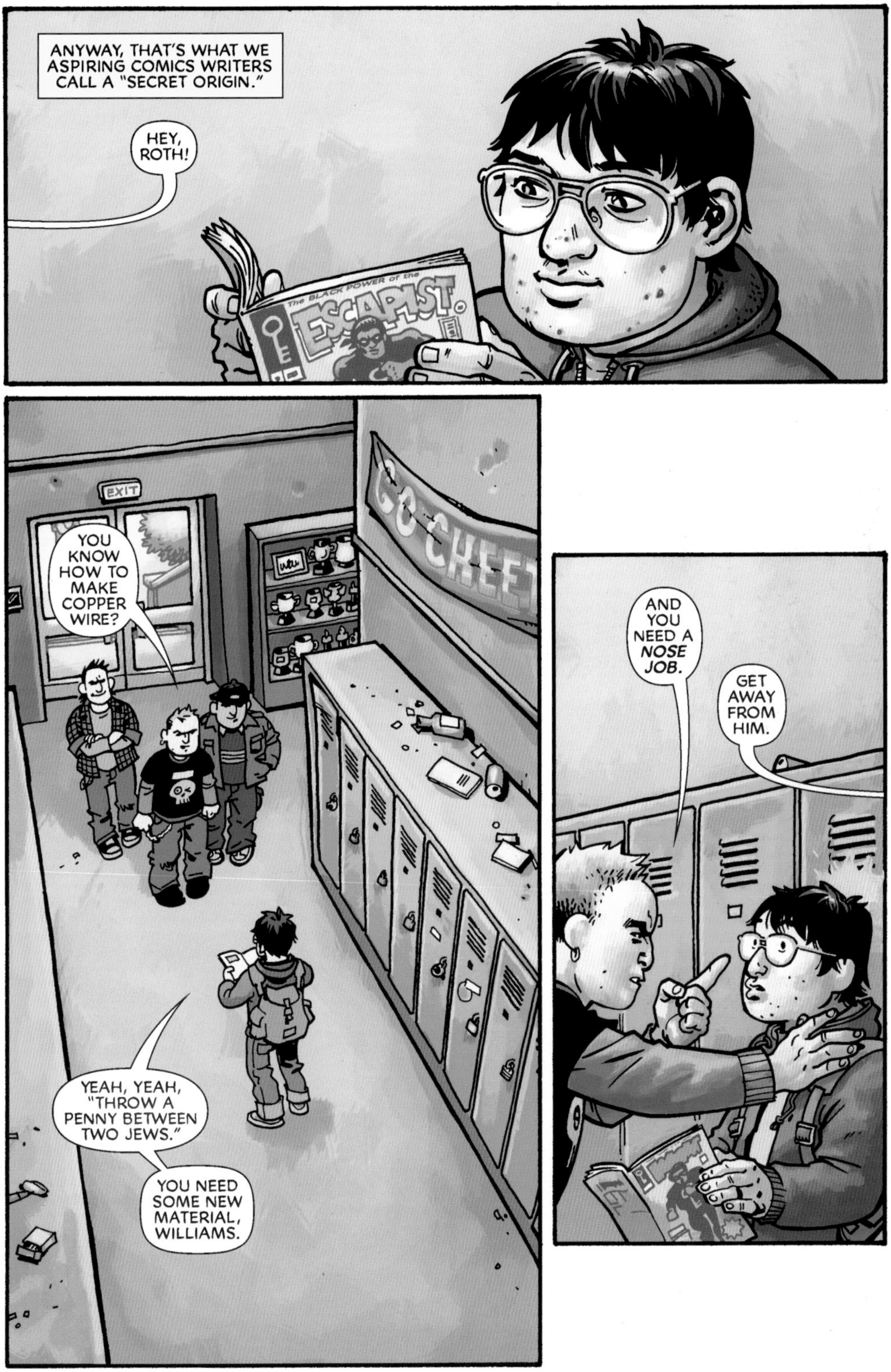
ANYWAY, THAT'S WHAT WE ASPIRING COMICS WRITERS CALL A "SECRET ORIGIN."
HEY, ROTH!
The BLACK POWER of the ESCAPIST
EXIT
GO CHEET
YOU KNOW HOW TO MAKE COPPER WIRE?
YEAH, YEAH, "THROW A PENNY BETWEEN TWO JEWS."
YOU NEED SOME NEW MATERIAL, WILLIAMS.
AND YOU NEED A *NOSE JOB.*
GET AWAY FROM HIM.

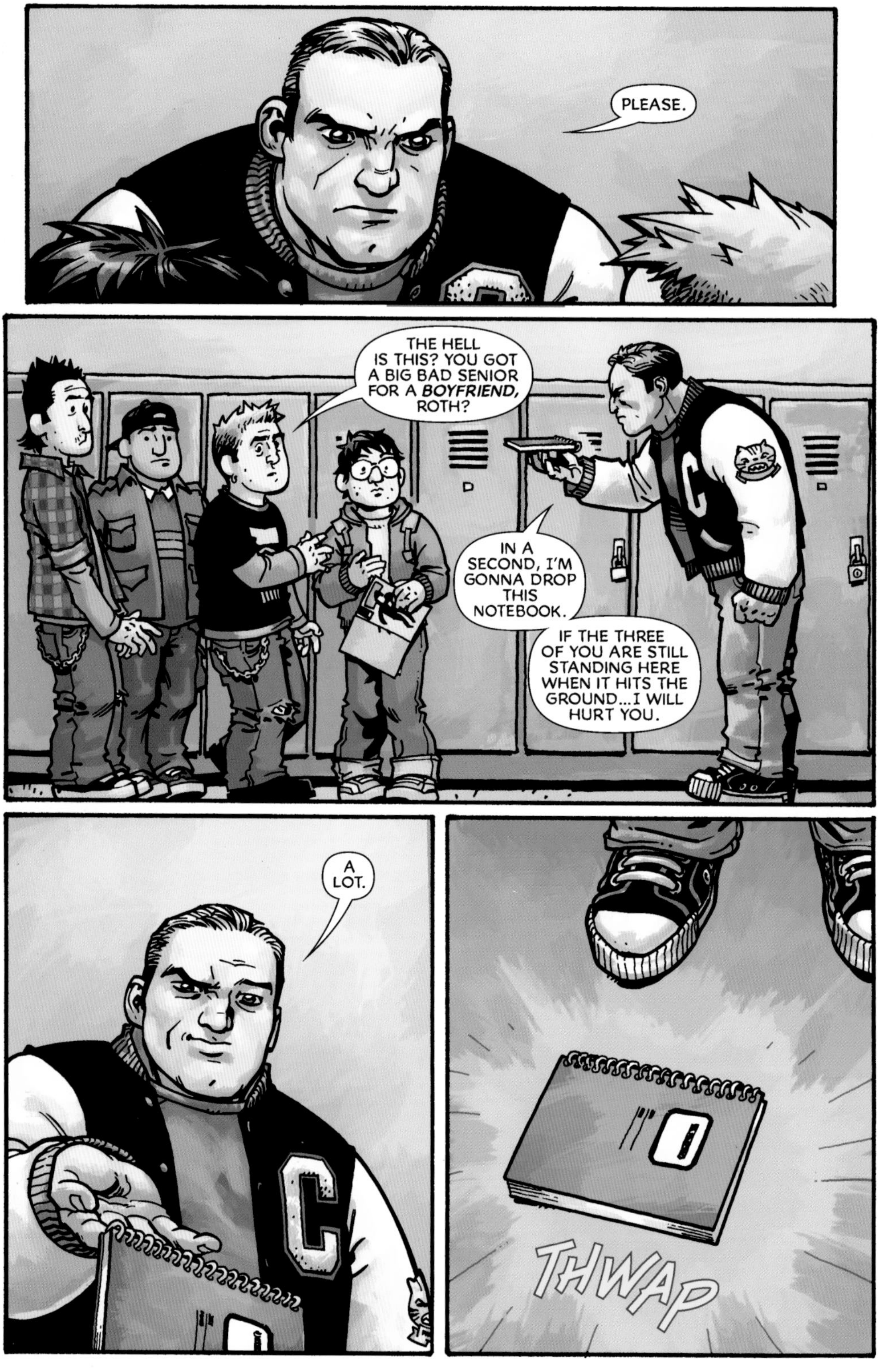
PLEASE.
THE HELL IS THIS? YOU GOT A BIG BAD SENIOR FOR A *BOYFRIEND,* ROTH?
IN A SECOND, I'M GONNA DROP THIS NOTEBOOK.
IF THE THREE OF YOU ARE STILL STANDING HERE WHEN IT HITS THE GROUND...I WILL HURT YOU.
A LOT.
THWAP

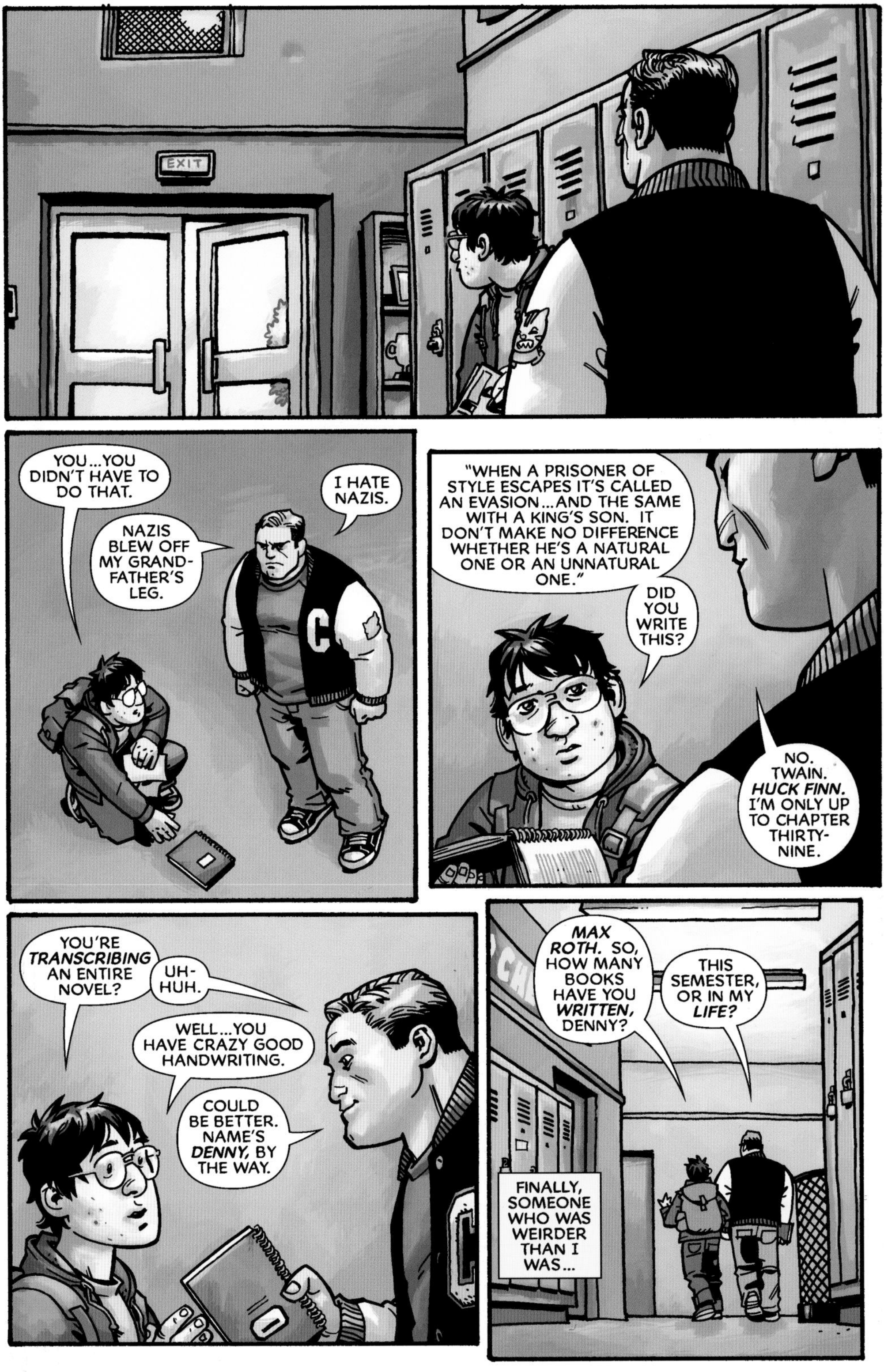
EXIT
YOU...YOU DIDN'T HAVE TO DO THAT.
I HATE NAZIS.
NAZIS BLEW OFF MY GRAND-FATHER'S LEG.
"WHEN A PRISONER OF STYLE ESCAPES IT'S CALLED AN EVASION...AND THE SAME WITH A KING'S SON. IT DON'T MAKE NO DIFFERENCE WHETHER HE'S A NATURAL ONE OR AN UNNATURAL ONE."
DID YOU WRITE THIS?
NO. TWAIN. *HUCK FINN.* I'M ONLY UP TO CHAPTER THIRTY-NINE.
YOU'RE *TRANSCRIBING* AN ENTIRE NOVEL?
UH-HUH.
WELL...YOU HAVE CRAZY GOOD HANDWRITING.
COULD BE BETTER. NAME'S *DENNY,* BY THE WAY.
MAX ROTH. SO, HOW MANY BOOKS HAVE YOU *WRITTEN,* DENNY?
THIS SEMESTER, OR IN MY *LIFE?*
FINALLY, SOMEONE WHO WAS WEIRDER THAN I WAS...

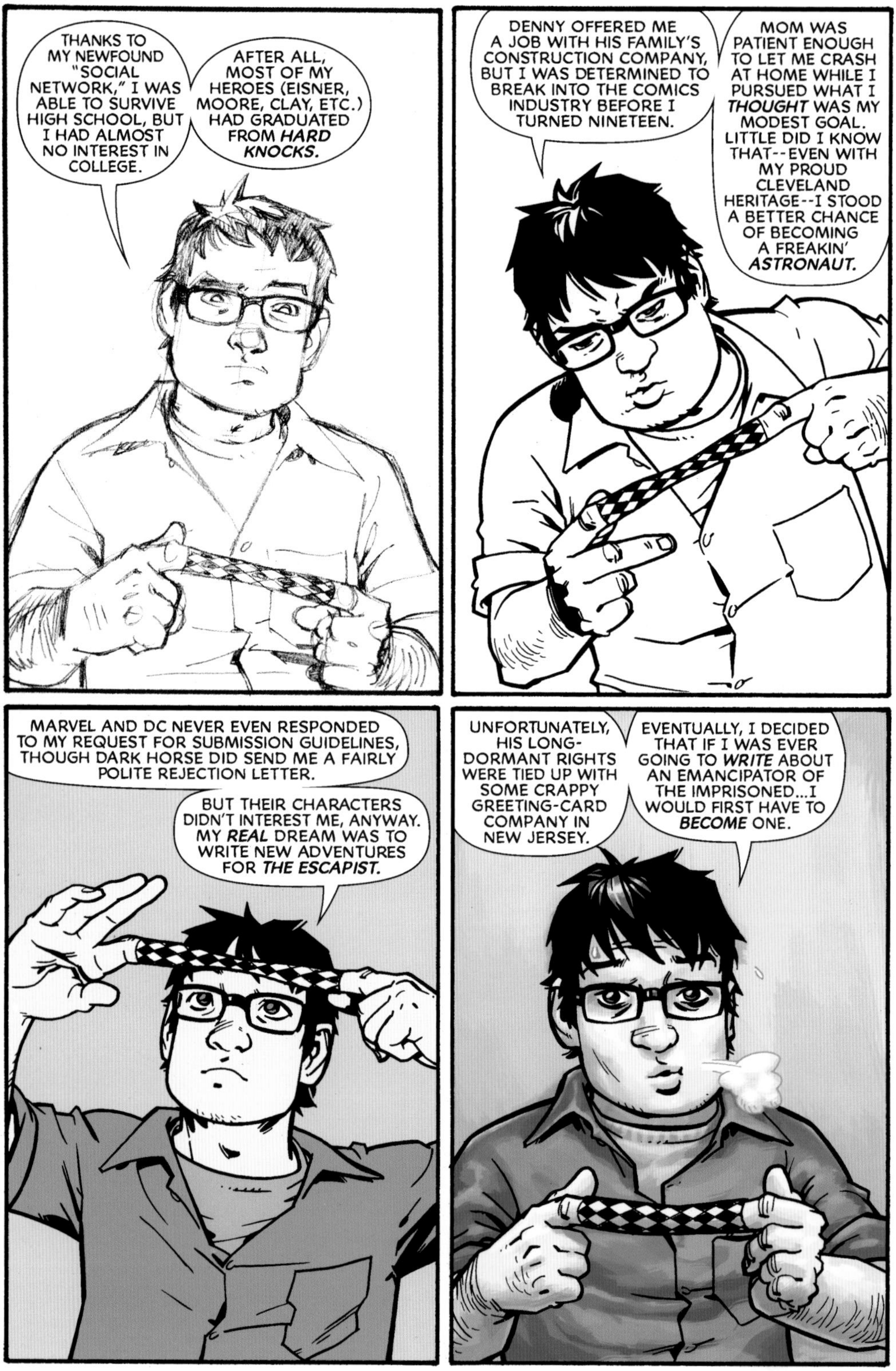
THANKS TO MY NEWFOUND "SOCIAL NETWORK," I WAS ABLE TO SURVIVE HIGH SCHOOL, BUT I HAD ALMOST NO INTEREST IN COLLEGE.
AFTER ALL, MOST OF MY HEROES (EISNER, MOORE, CLAY, ETC.) HAD GRADUATED FROM *HARD KNOCKS.*
DENNY OFFERED ME A JOB WITH HIS FAMILY'S CONSTRUCTION COMPANY, BUT I WAS DETERMINED TO BREAK INTO THE COMICS INDUSTRY BEFORE I TURNED NINETEEN.
MOM WAS PATIENT ENOUGH TO LET ME CRASH AT HOME WHILE I PURSUED WHAT I *THOUGHT* WAS MY MODEST GOAL. LITTLE DID I KNOW THAT--EVEN WITH MY PROUD CLEVELAND HERITAGE--I STOOD A BETTER CHANCE OF BECOMING A FREAKIN' *ASTRONAUT.*
MARVEL AND DC NEVER EVEN RESPONDED TO MY REQUEST FOR SUBMISSION GUIDELINES, THOUGH DARK HORSE DID SEND ME A FAIRLY POLITE REJECTION LETTER.
BUT THEIR CHARACTERS DIDN'T INTEREST ME, ANYWAY. MY *REAL* DREAM WAS TO WRITE NEW ADVENTURES FOR *THE ESCAPIST.*
UNFORTUNATELY, HIS LONG-DORMANT RIGHTS WERE TIED UP WITH SOME CRAPPY GREETING-CARD COMPANY IN NEW JERSEY.
EVENTUALLY, I DECIDED THAT IF I WAS EVER GOING TO *WRITE* ABOUT AN EMANCIPATOR OF THE IMPRISONED...I WOULD FIRST HAVE TO *BECOME* ONE.

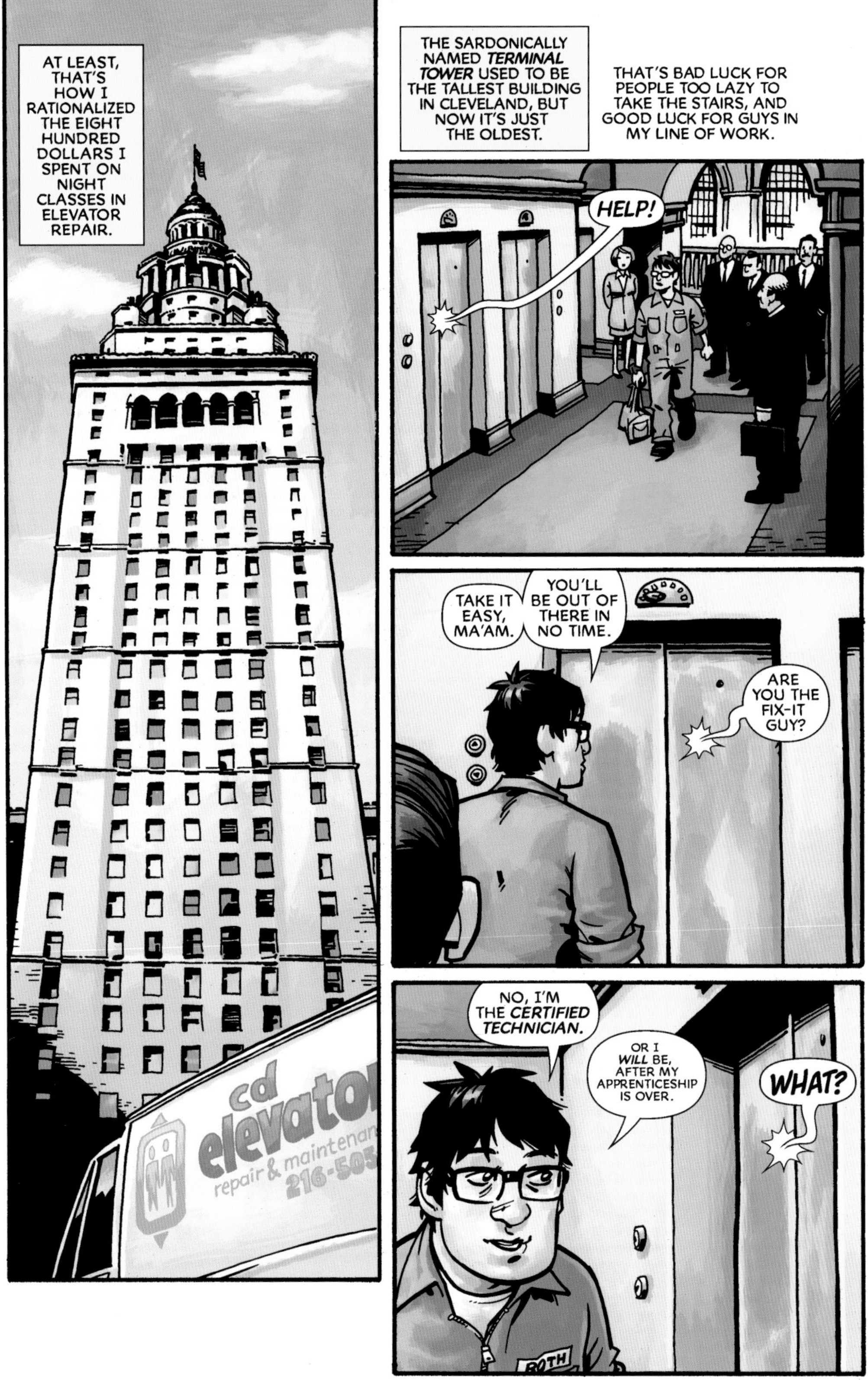
AT LEAST, THAT'S HOW I RATIONALIZED THE EIGHT HUNDRED DOLLARS I SPENT ON NIGHT CLASSES IN ELEVATOR REPAIR.
cd elevator repair & maintenan 216-505
THE SARDONICALLY NAMED *TERMINAL TOWER* USED TO BE THE TALLEST BUILDING IN CLEVELAND, BUT NOW IT'S JUST THE OLDEST.
THAT'S BAD LUCK FOR PEOPLE TOO LAZY TO TAKE THE STAIRS, AND GOOD LUCK FOR GUYS IN MY LINE OF WORK.
HELP!
TAKE IT EASY, MA'AM.
YOU'LL BE OUT OF THERE IN NO TIME.
ARE YOU THE FIX-IT GUY?
NO, I'M THE *CERTIFIED TECHNICIAN.*
OR I *WILL* BE, AFTER MY APPRENTICESHIP IS OVER.
WHAT?
ROTH

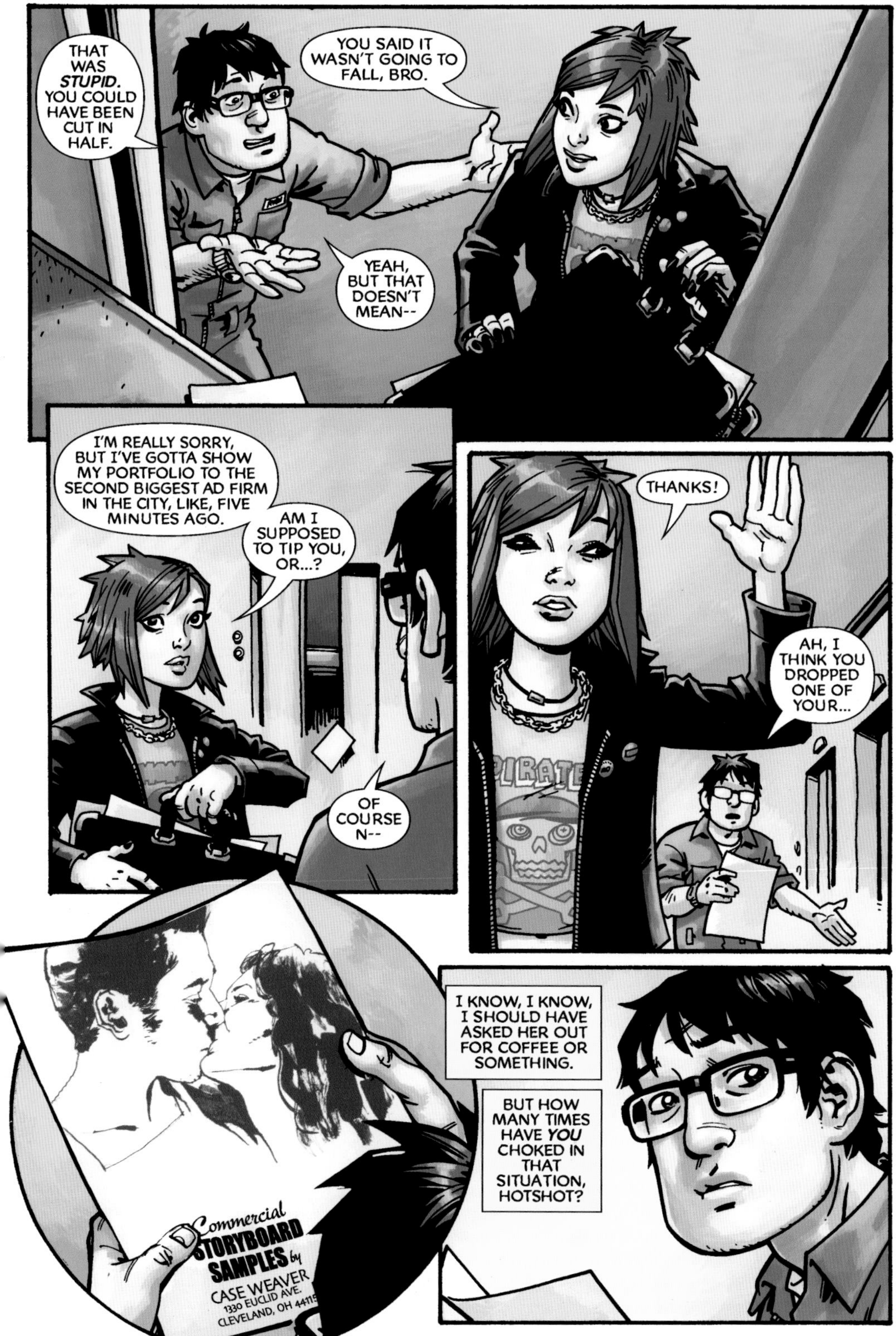
THAT WAS *STUPID*. YOU COULD HAVE BEEN CUT IN HALF.
YOU SAID IT WASN'T GOING TO FALL, BRO.
YEAH, BUT THAT DOESN'T MEAN--
I'M REALLY SORRY, BUT I'VE GOTTA SHOW MY PORTFOLIO TO THE SECOND BIGGEST AD FIRM IN THE CITY, LIKE, FIVE MINUTES AGO.
AM I SUPPOSED TO TIP YOU, OR...?
OF COURSE N--
THANKS!
AH, I THINK YOU DROPPED ONE OF YOUR...
Commercial STORYBOARD SAMPLES by
CASE WEAVER
1330 EUCLID AVE.
CLEVELAND, OH 44115
I KNOW, I KNOW, I SHOULD HAVE ASKED HER OUT FOR COFFEE OR SOMETHING.
BUT HOW MANY TIMES HAVE *YOU* CHOKED IN THAT SITUATION, HOTSHOT?

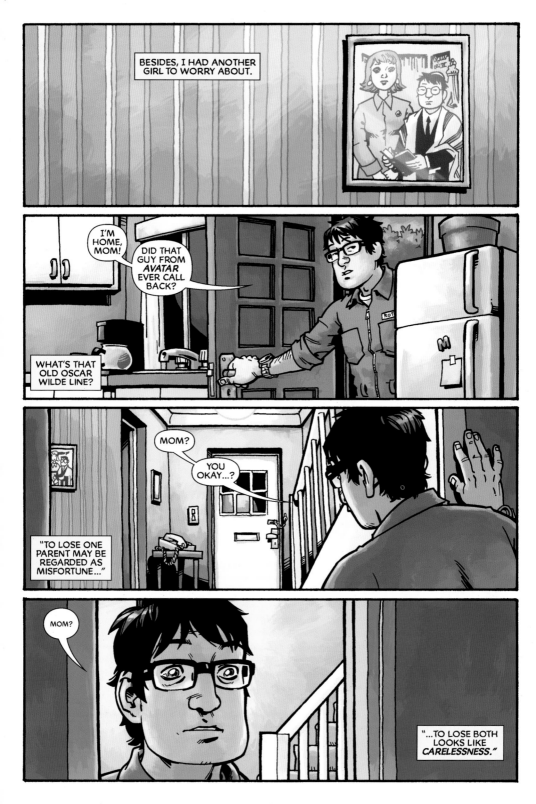

BESIDES, I HAD ANOTHER GIRL TO WORRY ABOUT.

I'M HOME, MOM!

DID THAT GUY FROM *AVATAR* EVER CALL BACK?

WHAT'S THAT OLD OSCAR WILDE LINE?

MOM?

YOU OKAY...?

"TO LOSE ONE PARENT MAY BE REGARDED AS MISFORTUNE..."

MOM?

"...TO LOSE BOTH LOOKS LIKE *CARELESSNESS.*"

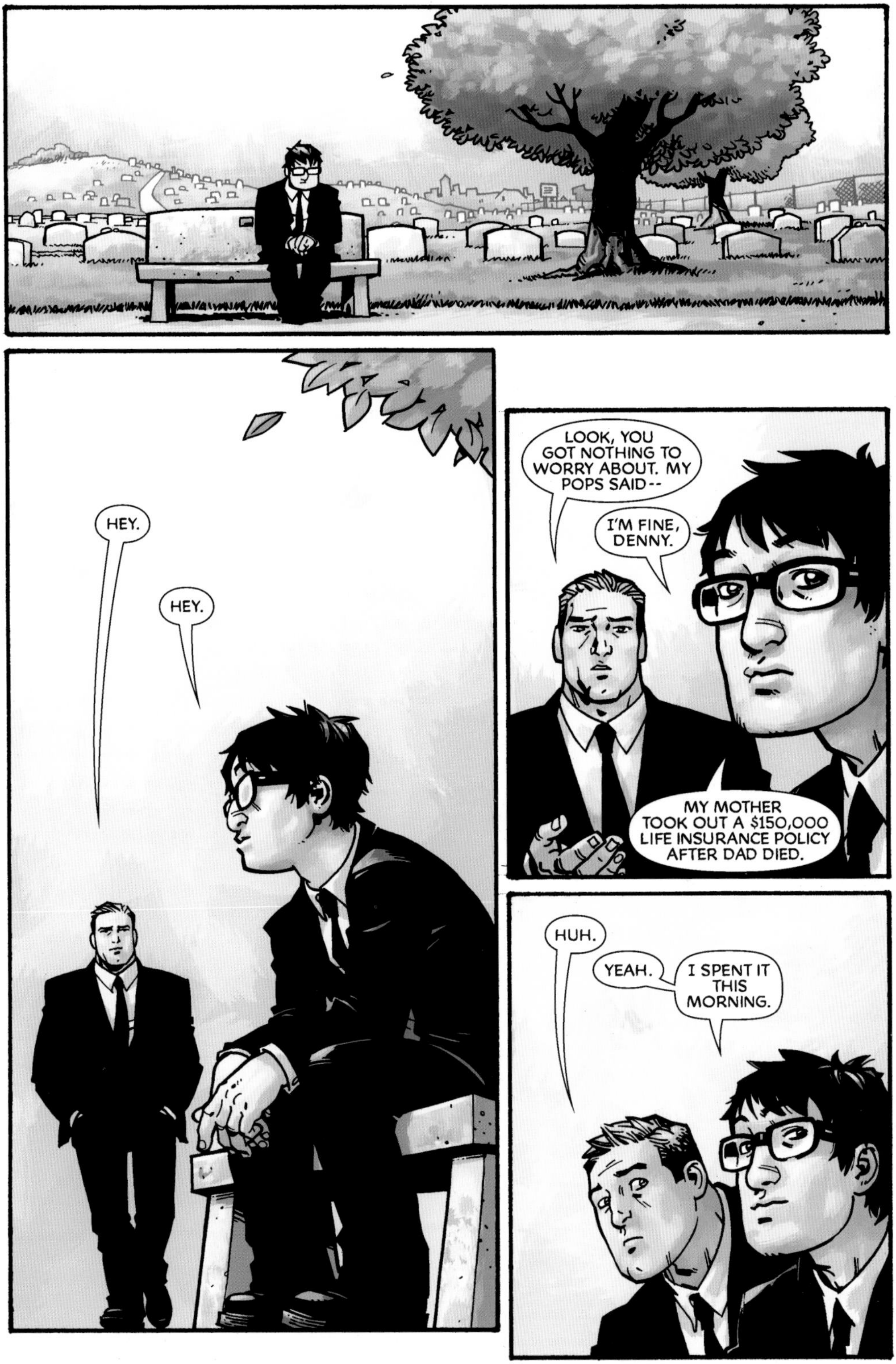
HEY.
HEY.
LOOK, YOU GOT NOTHING TO WORRY ABOUT. MY POPS SAID--
I'M FINE, DENNY.
MY MOTHER TOOK OUT A $150,000 LIFE INSURANCE POLICY AFTER DAD DIED.
HUH.
YEAH.
I SPENT IT THIS MORNING.

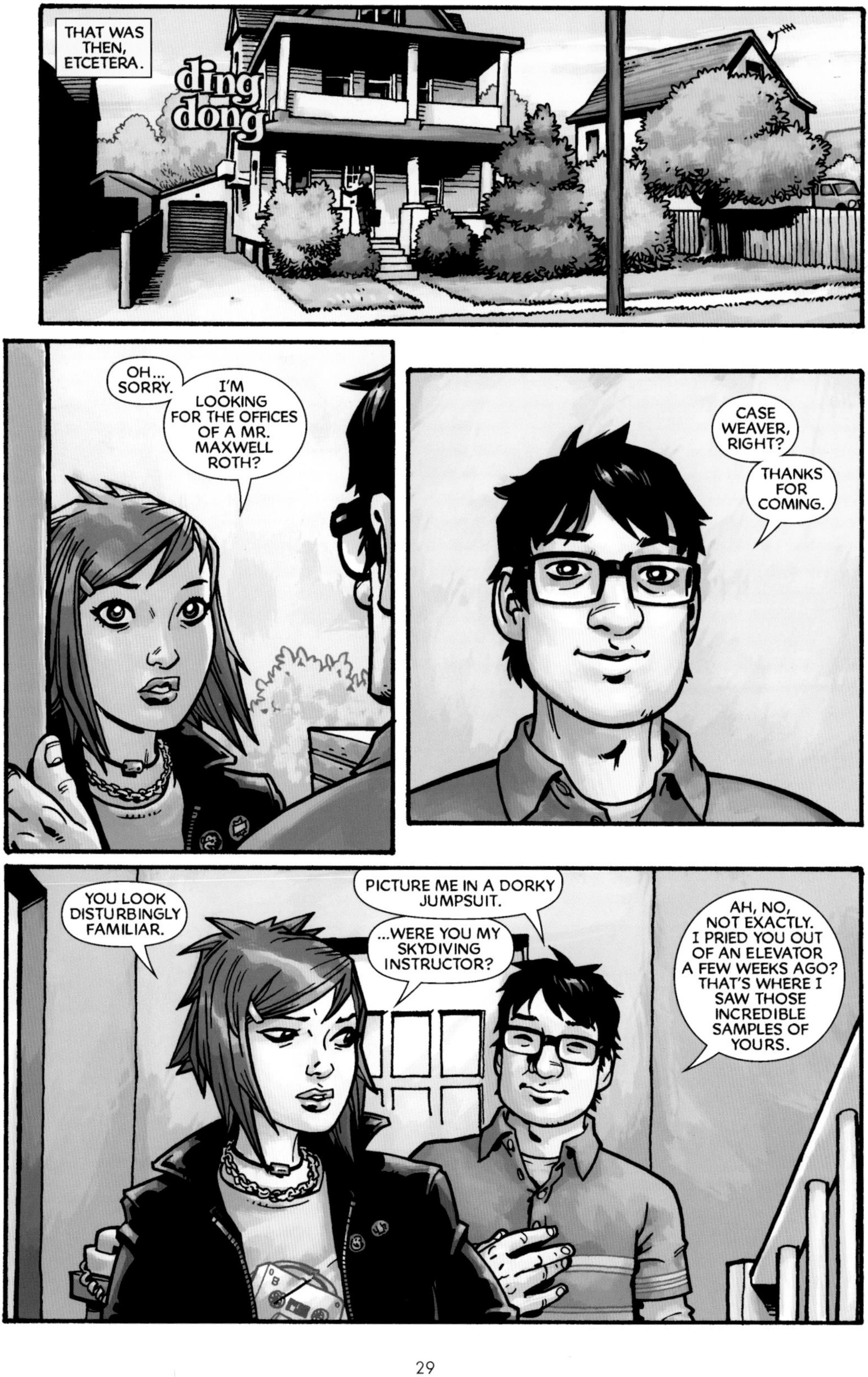
THAT WAS THEN, ETCETERA.
ding dong
OH... SORRY.
I'M LOOKING FOR THE OFFICES OF A MR. MAXWELL ROTH?
CASE WEAVER, RIGHT?
THANKS FOR COMING.
YOU LOOK DISTURBINGLY FAMILIAR.
PICTURE ME IN A DORKY JUMPSUIT.
...WERE YOU MY SKYDIVING INSTRUCTOR?
AH, NO, NOT EXACTLY. I PRIED YOU OUT OF AN ELEVATOR A FEW WEEKS AGO? THAT'S WHERE I SAW THOSE INCREDIBLE SAMPLES OF YOURS.

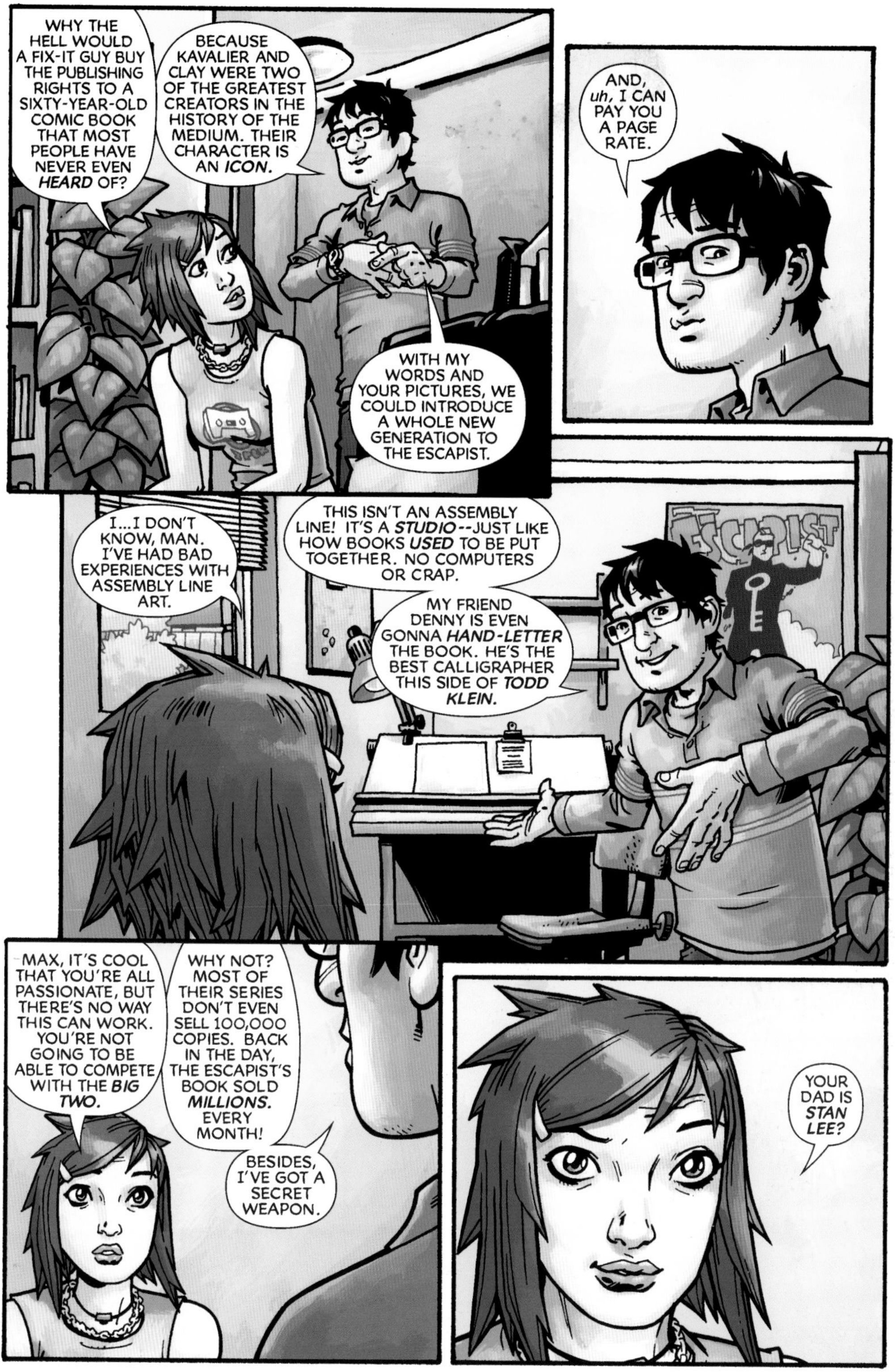
WHY THE HELL WOULD A FIX-IT GUY BUY THE PUBLISHING RIGHTS TO A SIXTY-YEAR-OLD COMIC BOOK THAT MOST PEOPLE HAVE NEVER EVEN *HEARD* OF?
BECAUSE KAVALIER AND CLAY WERE TWO OF THE GREATEST CREATORS IN THE HISTORY OF THE MEDIUM. THEIR CHARACTER IS AN *ICON*.
WITH MY WORDS AND YOUR PICTURES, WE COULD INTRODUCE A WHOLE NEW GENERATION TO THE ESCAPIST.
AND, *uh*, I CAN PAY YOU A PAGE RATE.
I...I DON'T KNOW, MAN. I'VE HAD BAD EXPERIENCES WITH ASSEMBLY LINE ART.
THIS ISN'T AN ASSEMBLY LINE! IT'S A *STUDIO*--JUST LIKE HOW BOOKS *USED* TO BE PUT TOGETHER. NO COMPUTERS OR CRAP.
MY FRIEND DENNY IS EVEN GONNA *HAND-LETTER* THE BOOK. HE'S THE BEST CALLIGRAPHER THIS SIDE OF *TODD KLEIN*.
ESCAPIST
MAX, IT'S COOL THAT YOU'RE ALL PASSIONATE, BUT THERE'S NO WAY THIS CAN WORK. YOU'RE NOT GOING TO BE ABLE TO COMPETE WITH THE *BIG TWO*.
WHY NOT? MOST OF THEIR SERIES DON'T EVEN SELL 100,000 COPIES. BACK IN THE DAY, THE ESCAPIST'S BOOK SOLD *MILLIONS*. EVERY MONTH!
BESIDES, I'VE GOT A SECRET WEAPON.
YOUR DAD IS *STAN LEE?*

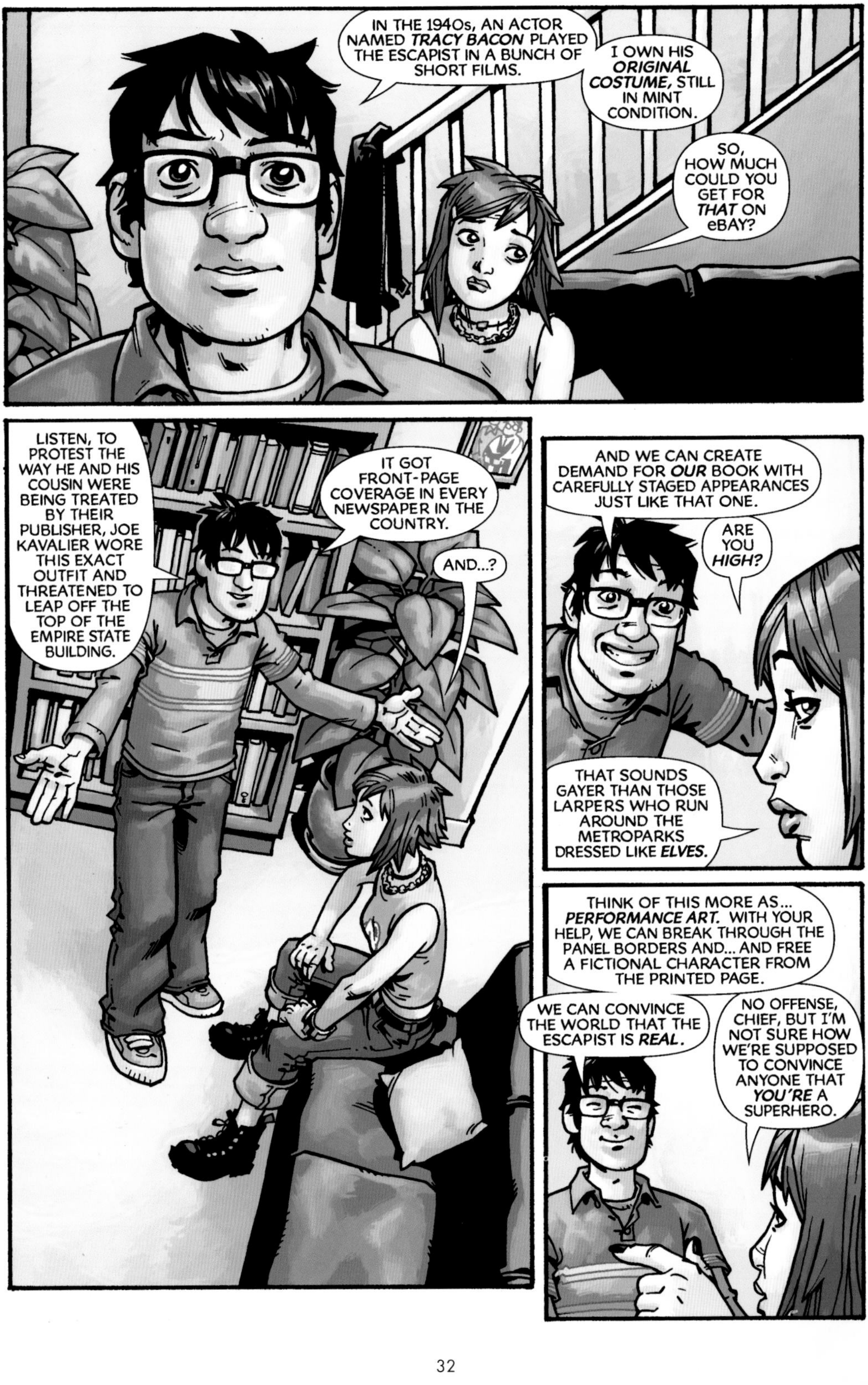
IN THE 1940s, AN ACTOR NAMED TRACY BACON PLAYED THE ESCAPIST IN A BUNCH OF SHORT FILMS.
I OWN HIS ORIGINAL COSTUME, STILL IN MINT CONDITION.
SO, HOW MUCH COULD YOU GET FOR THAT ON eBAY?
LISTEN, TO PROTEST THE WAY HE AND HIS COUSIN WERE BEING TREATED BY THEIR PUBLISHER, JOE KAVALIER WORE THIS EXACT OUTFIT AND THREATENED TO LEAP OFF THE TOP OF THE EMPIRE STATE BUILDING.
IT GOT FRONT-PAGE COVERAGE IN EVERY NEWSPAPER IN THE COUNTRY.
AND...?
AND WE CAN CREATE DEMAND FOR OUR BOOK WITH CAREFULLY STAGED APPEARANCES JUST LIKE THAT ONE.
ARE YOU HIGH?
THAT SOUNDS GAYER THAN THOSE LARPERS WHO RUN AROUND THE METROPARKS DRESSED LIKE ELVES.
THINK OF THIS MORE AS... PERFORMANCE ART. WITH YOUR HELP, WE CAN BREAK THROUGH THE PANEL BORDERS AND... AND FREE A FICTIONAL CHARACTER FROM THE PRINTED PAGE.
WE CAN CONVINCE THE WORLD THAT THE ESCAPIST IS REAL.
NO OFFENSE, CHIEF, BUT I'M NOT SURE HOW WE'RE SUPPOSED TO CONVINCE ANYONE THAT YOU'RE A SUPERHERO.

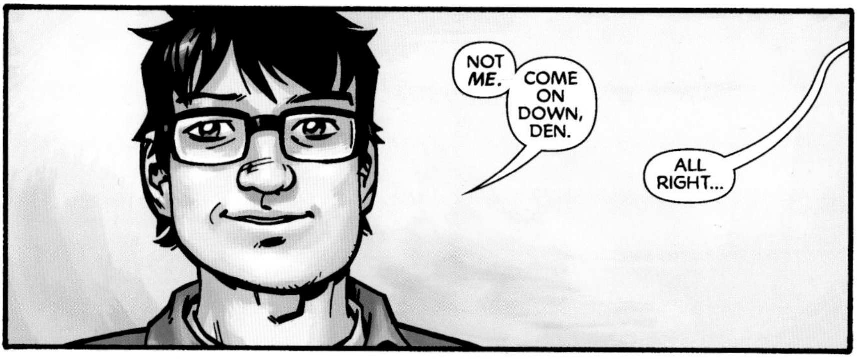
NOT *ME.*
COME ON DOWN, DEN.
ALL RIGHT...

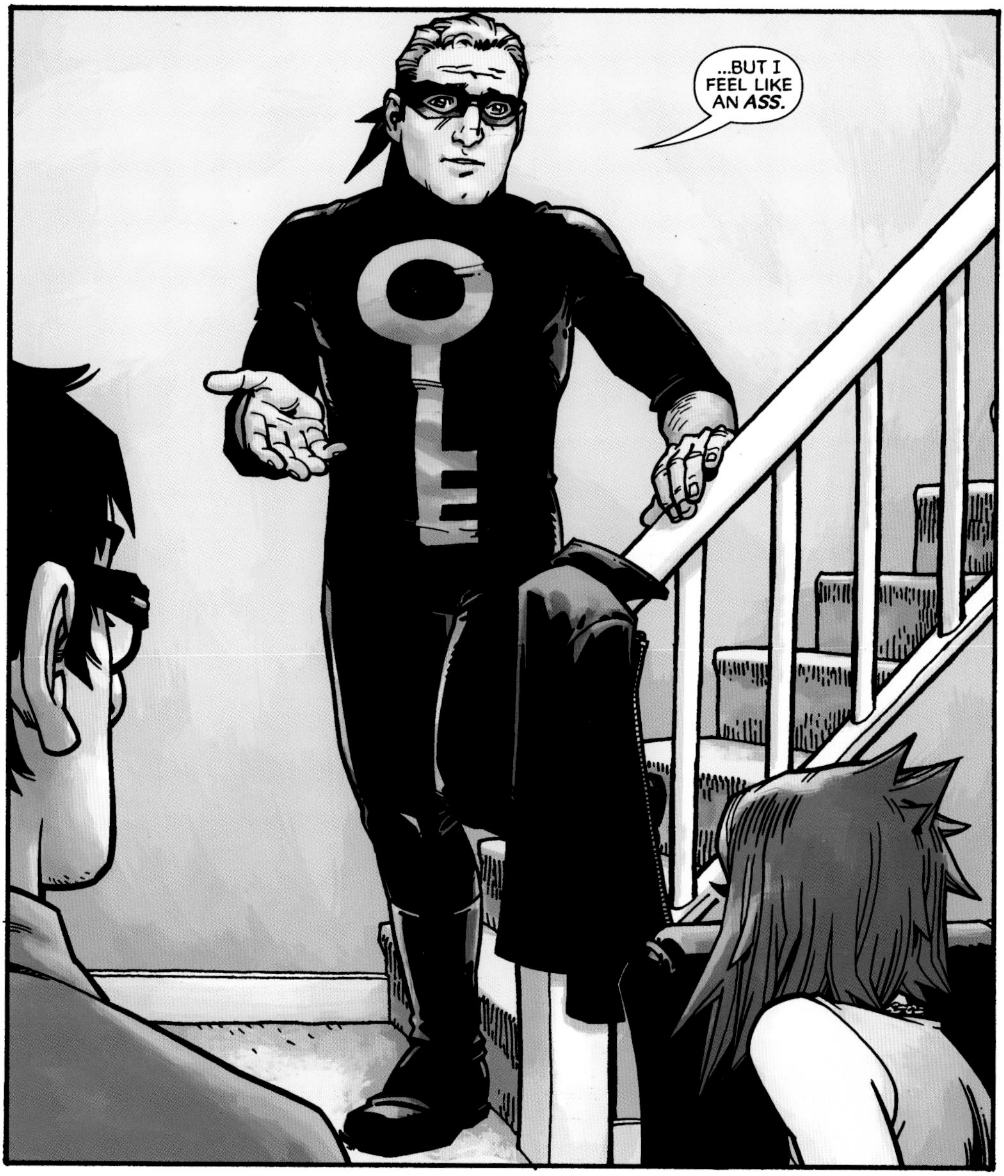
...BUT I FEEL LIKE AN *ASS.*

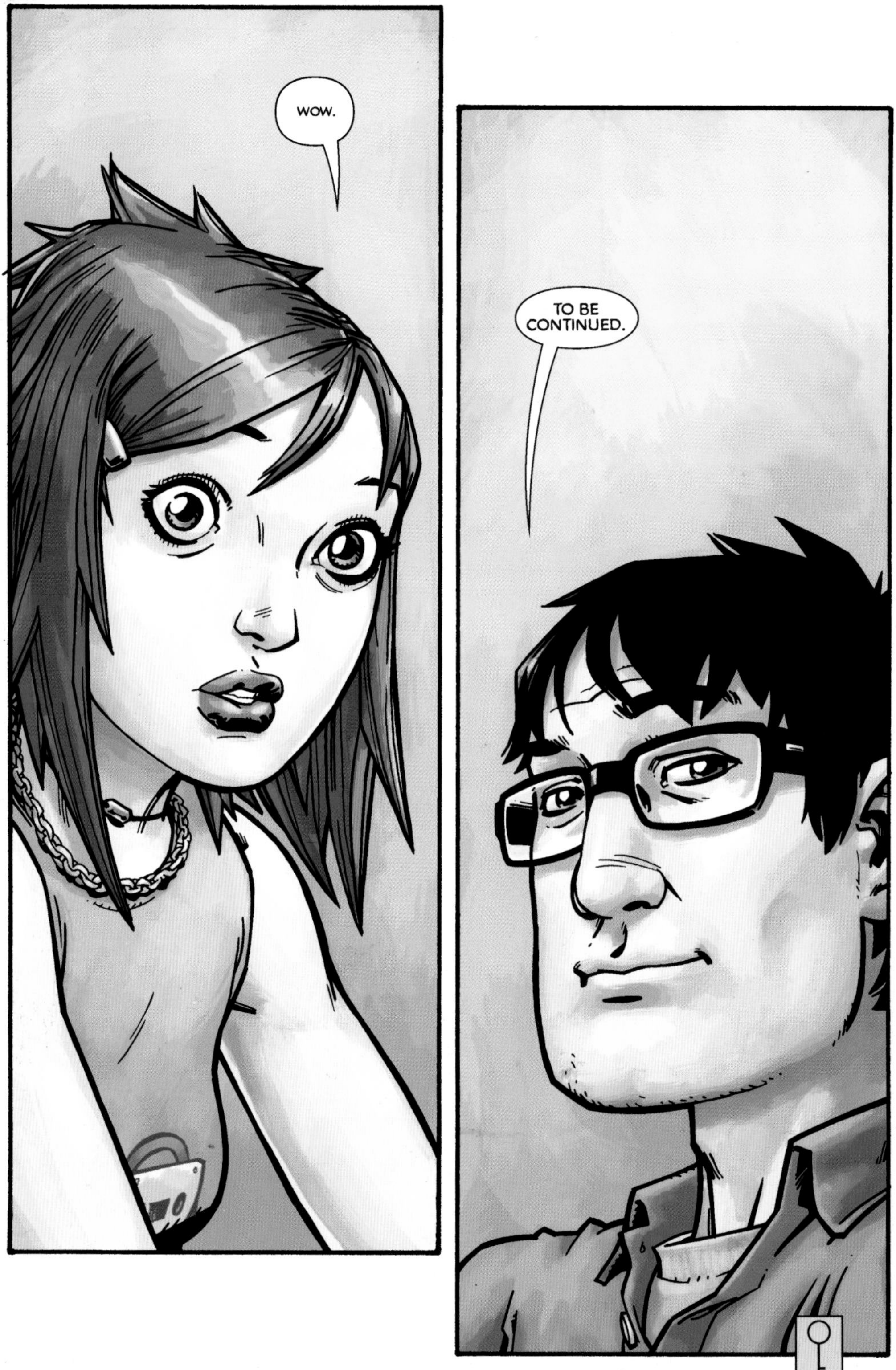
WOW.
TO BE CONTINUED.

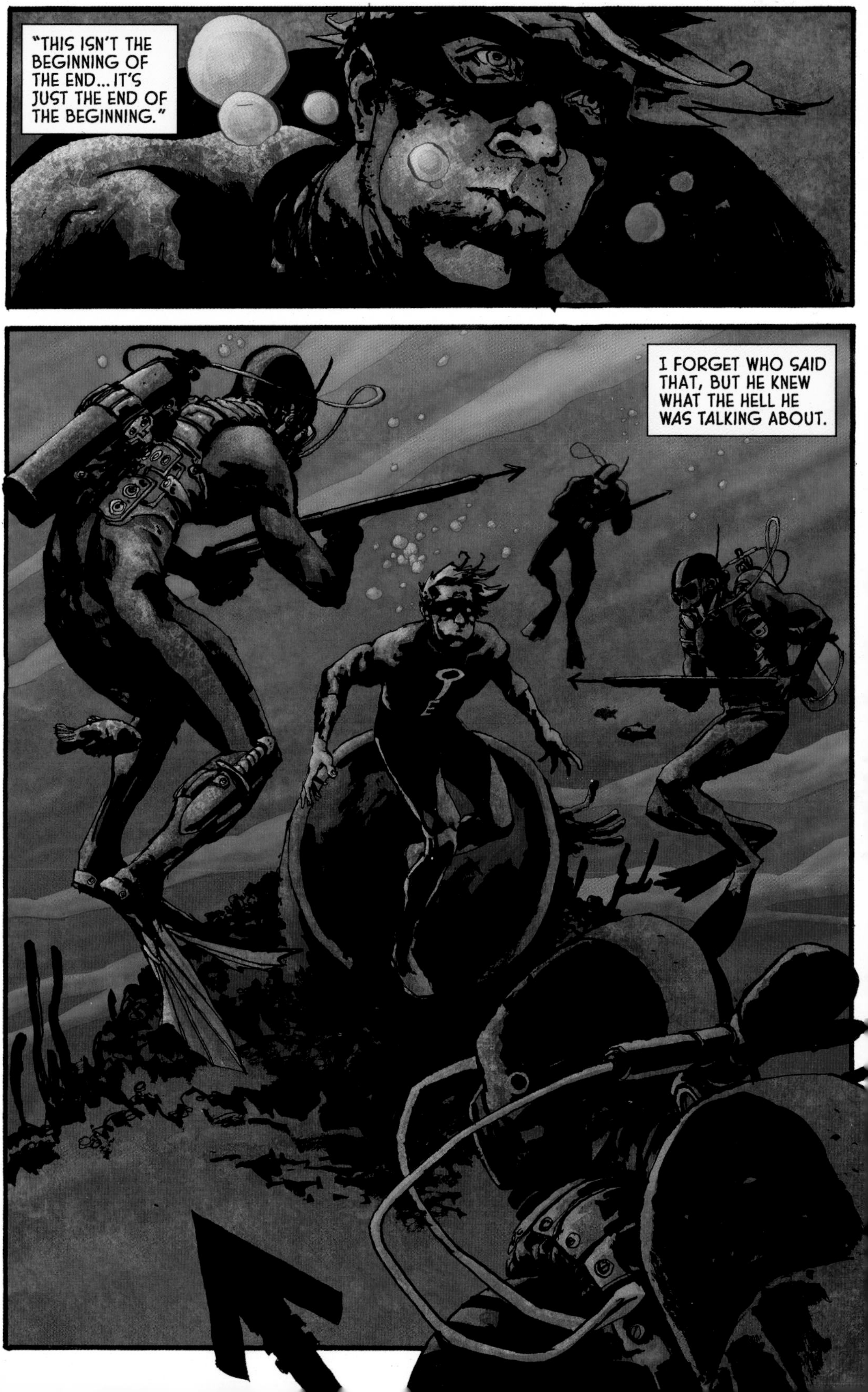
"THIS ISN'T THE BEGINNING OF THE END... IT'S JUST THE END OF THE BEGINNING."
I FORGET WHO SAID THAT, BUT HE KNEW WHAT THE HELL HE WAS TALKING ABOUT.

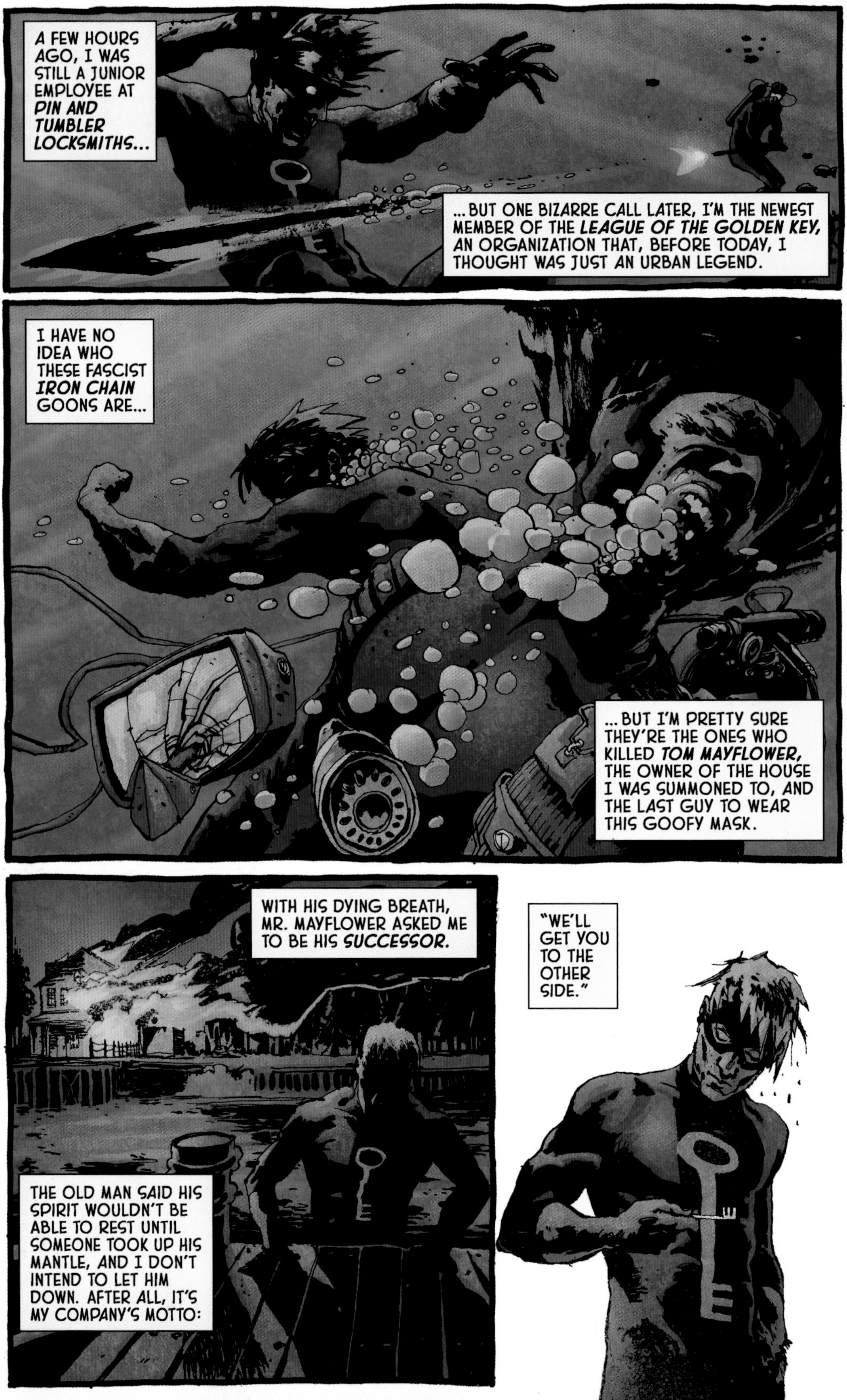
A FEW HOURS AGO, I WAS STILL A JUNIOR EMPLOYEE AT PIN AND TUMBLER LOCKSMITHS...
...BUT ONE BIZARRE CALL LATER, I'M THE NEWEST MEMBER OF THE LEAGUE OF THE GOLDEN KEY, AN ORGANIZATION THAT, BEFORE TODAY, I THOUGHT WAS JUST AN URBAN LEGEND.
I HAVE NO IDEA WHO THESE FASCIST IRON CHAIN GOONS ARE...
...BUT I'M PRETTY SURE THEY'RE THE ONES WHO KILLED TOM MAYFLOWER, THE OWNER OF THE HOUSE I WAS SUMMONED TO, AND THE LAST GUY TO WEAR THIS GOOFY MASK.
WITH HIS DYING BREATH, MR. MAYFLOWER ASKED ME TO BE HIS SUCCESSOR.
THE OLD MAN SAID HIS SPIRIT WOULDN'T BE ABLE TO REST UNTIL SOMEONE TOOK UP HIS MANTLE, AND I DON'T INTEND TO LET HIM DOWN. AFTER ALL, IT'S MY COMPANY'S MOTTO:
"WE'LL GET YOU TO THE OTHER SIDE."

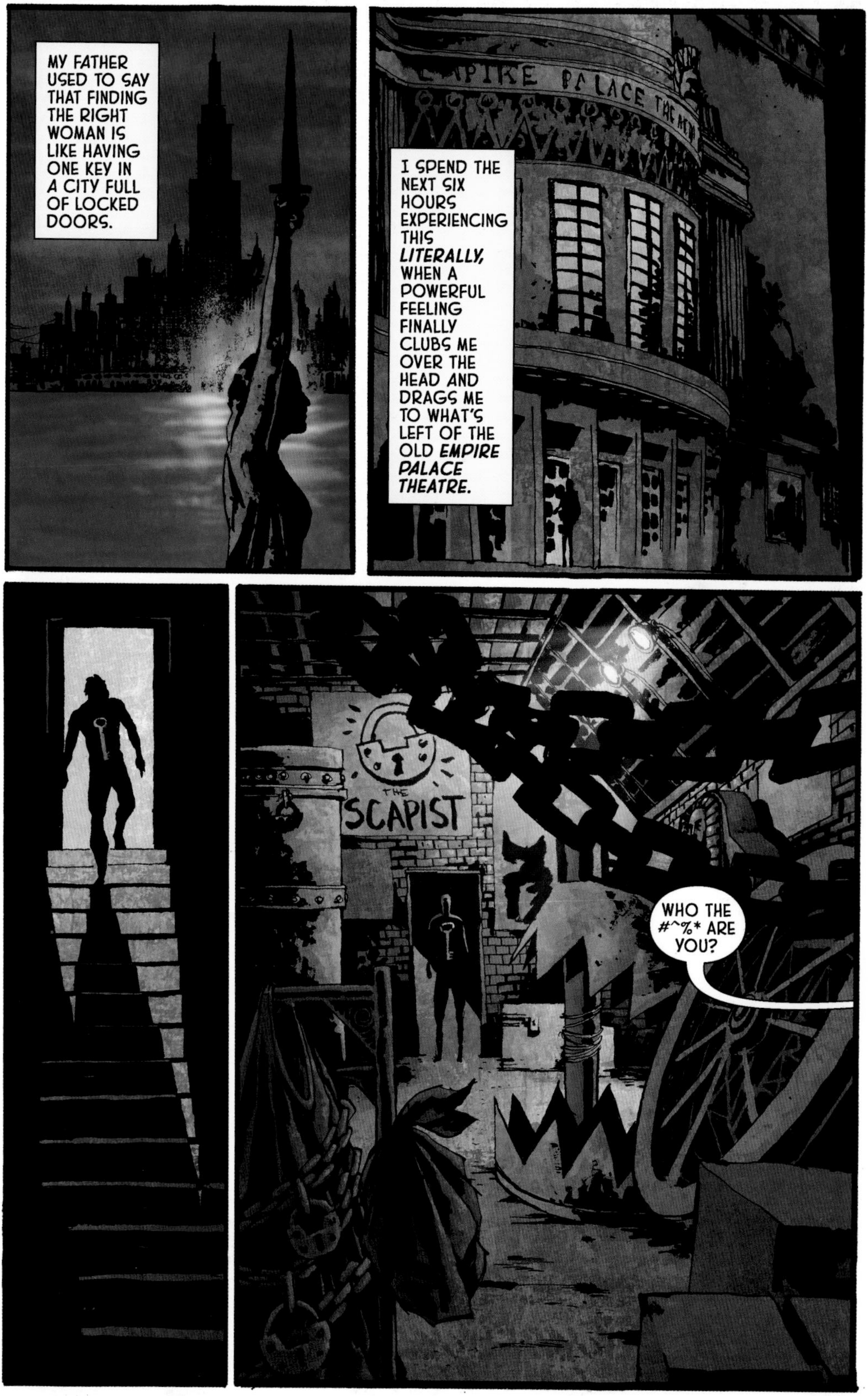
MY FATHER USED TO SAY THAT FINDING THE RIGHT WOMAN IS LIKE HAVING ONE KEY IN A CITY FULL OF LOCKED DOORS.
I SPEND THE NEXT SIX HOURS EXPERIENCING THIS *LITERALLY,* WHEN A POWERFUL FEELING FINALLY CLUBS ME OVER THE HEAD AND DRAGS ME TO WHAT'S LEFT OF THE OLD *EMPIRE PALACE THEATRE.*
THE SCAPIST
WHO THE #^%* ARE YOU?

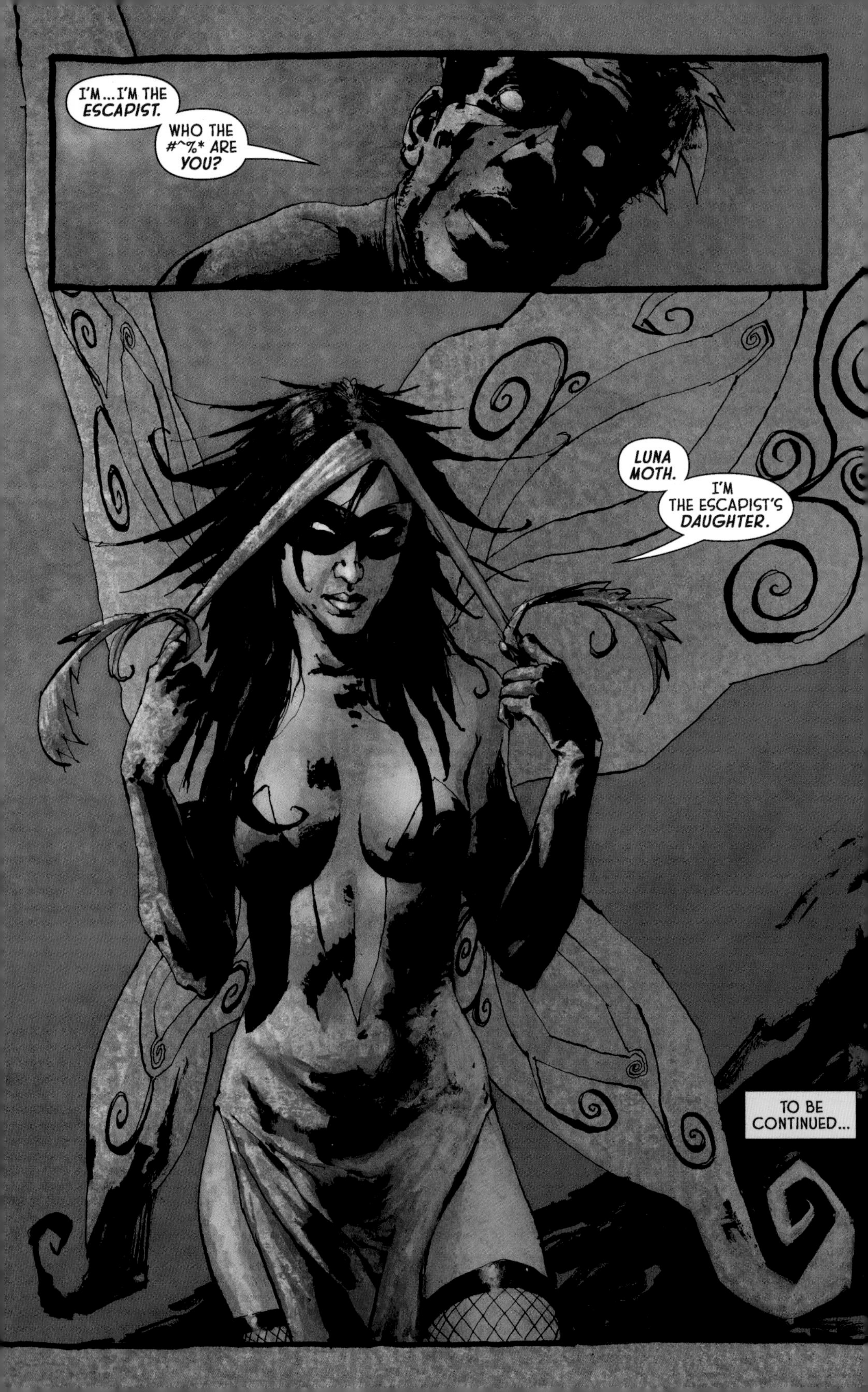

I'M...I'M THE ESCAPIST.
WHO THE #^%* ARE YOU?
LUNA MOTH.
I'M THE ESCAPIST'S DAUGHTER.
TO BE CONTINUED...

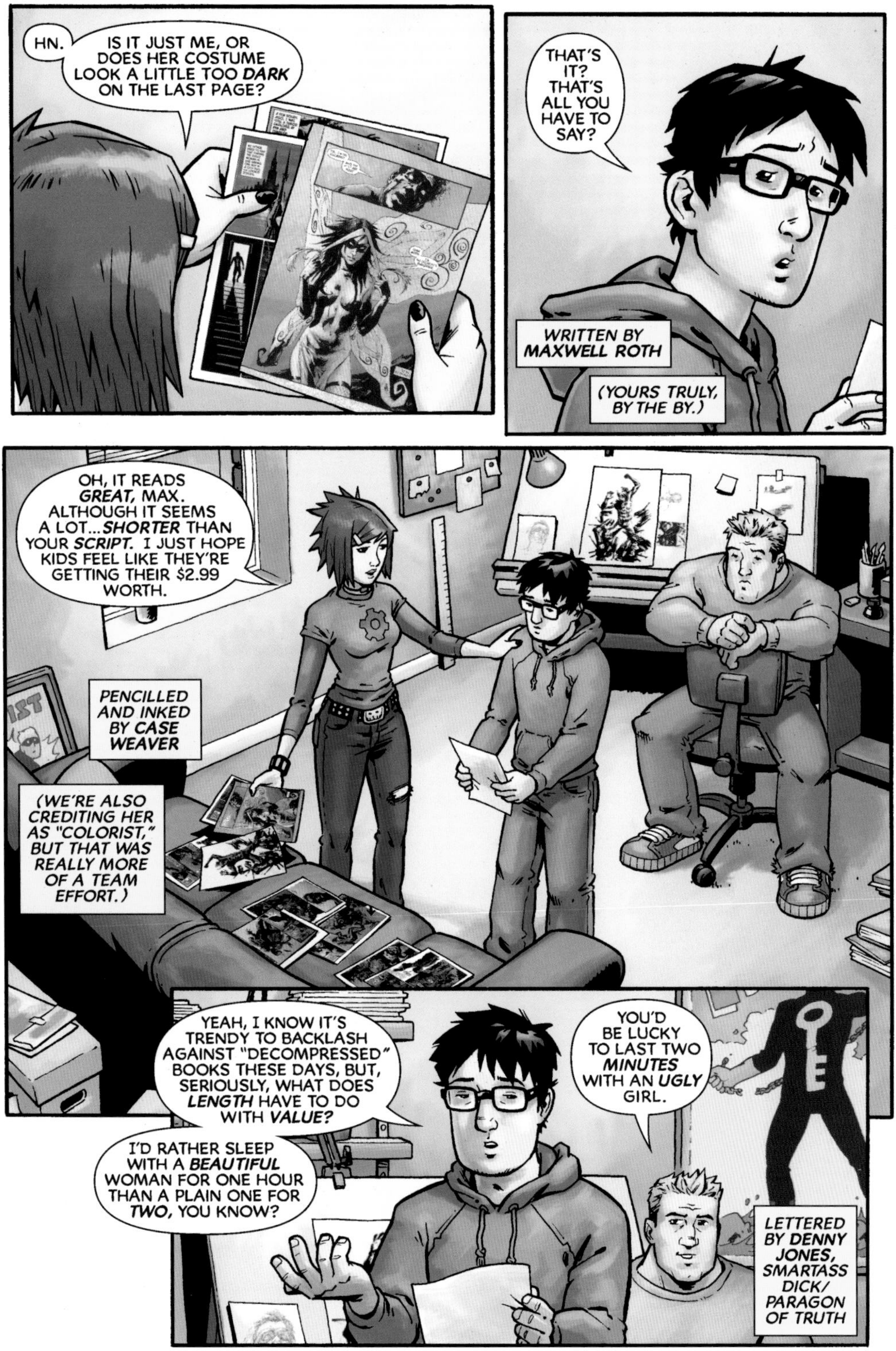
HN.
IS IT JUST ME, OR DOES HER COSTUME LOOK A LITTLE TOO *DARK* ON THE LAST PAGE?
THAT'S IT? THAT'S ALL YOU HAVE TO SAY?
WRITTEN BY **MAXWELL ROTH**
(YOURS TRULY, BY THE BY.)
OH, IT READS **GREAT,** MAX. ALTHOUGH IT SEEMS A LOT...**SHORTER** THAN YOUR **SCRIPT.** I JUST HOPE KIDS FEEL LIKE THEY'RE GETTING THEIR $2.99 WORTH.
PENCILLED AND INKED BY **CASE WEAVER**
(WE'RE ALSO CREDITING HER AS "COLORIST," BUT THAT WAS REALLY MORE OF A TEAM EFFORT.)
YEAH, I KNOW IT'S TRENDY TO BACKLASH AGAINST "DECOMPRESSED" BOOKS THESE DAYS, BUT, SERIOUSLY, WHAT DOES **LENGTH** HAVE TO DO WITH **VALUE?**
I'D RATHER SLEEP WITH A **BEAUTIFUL** WOMAN FOR ONE HOUR THAN A PLAIN ONE FOR **TWO,** YOU KNOW?
YOU'D BE LUCKY TO LAST TWO **MINUTES** WITH AN **UGLY** GIRL.
LETTERED BY **DENNY JONES,** SMARTASS DICK/ PARAGON OF TRUTH

41

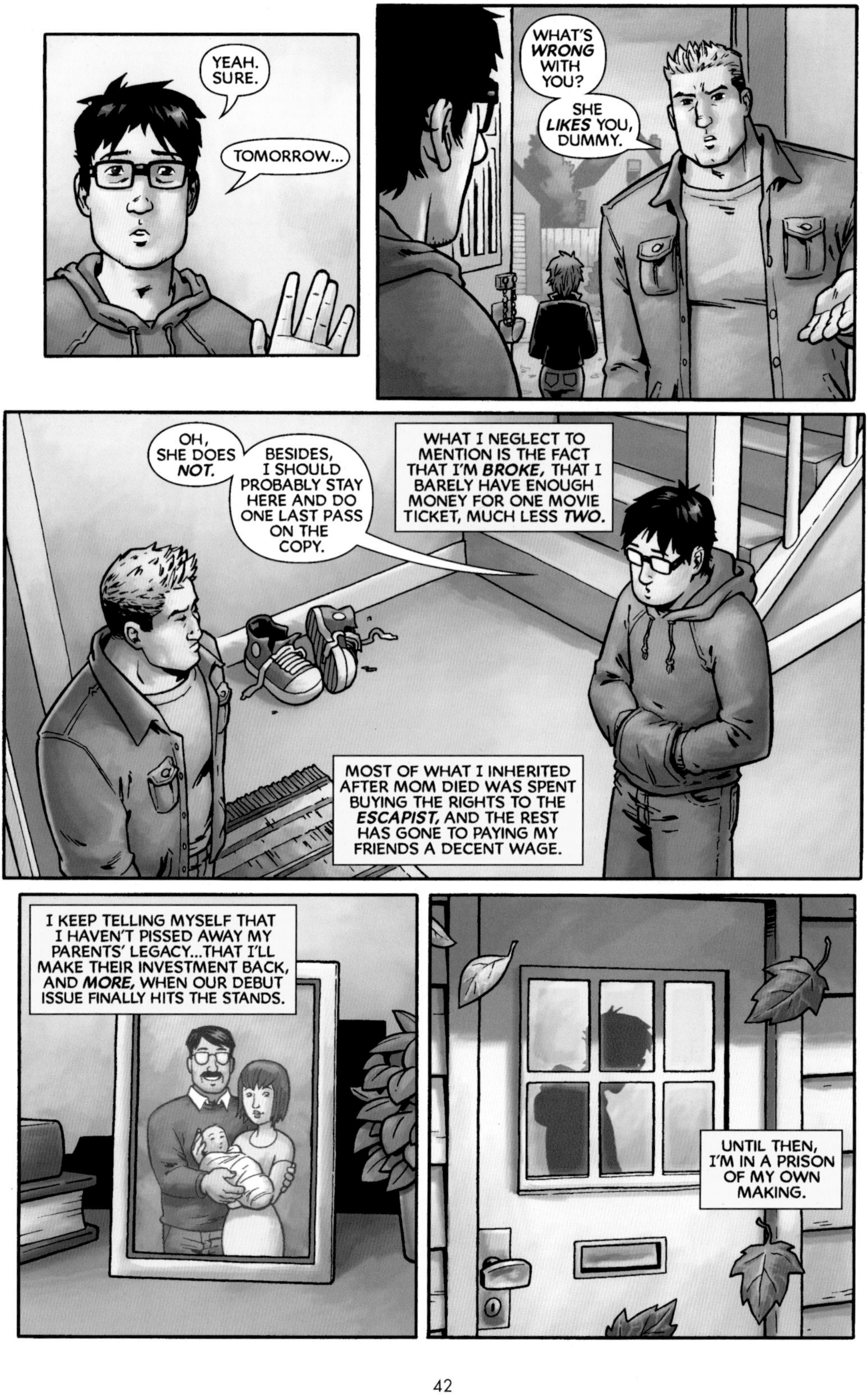

YEAH. SURE.
TOMORROW...
WHAT'S **WRONG** WITH YOU?
SHE **LIKES** YOU, DUMMY.
OH, SHE DOES **NOT.**
BESIDES, I SHOULD PROBABLY STAY HERE AND DO ONE LAST PASS ON THE COPY.
WHAT I NEGLECT TO MENTION IS THE FACT THAT I'M **BROKE,** THAT I BARELY HAVE ENOUGH MONEY FOR ONE MOVIE TICKET, MUCH LESS **TWO.**
MOST OF WHAT I INHERITED AFTER MOM DIED WAS SPENT BUYING THE RIGHTS TO THE ***ESCAPIST,*** AND THE REST HAS GONE TO PAYING MY FRIENDS A DECENT WAGE.
I KEEP TELLING MYSELF THAT I HAVEN'T PISSED AWAY MY PARENTS' LEGACY...THAT I'LL MAKE THEIR INVESTMENT BACK, AND ***MORE,*** WHEN OUR DEBUT ISSUE FINALLY HITS THE STANDS.
UNTIL THEN, I'M IN A PRISON OF MY OWN MAKING.

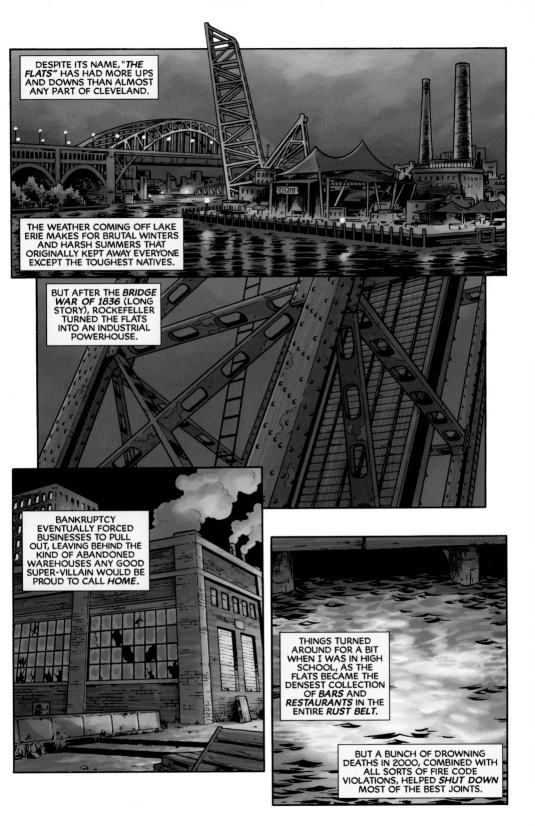

DESPITE ITS NAME, "*THE FLATS*" HAS HAD MORE UPS AND DOWNS THAN ALMOST ANY PART OF CLEVELAND.

THE WEATHER COMING OFF LAKE ERIE MAKES FOR BRUTAL WINTERS AND HARSH SUMMERS THAT ORIGINALLY KEPT AWAY EVERYONE EXCEPT THE TOUGHEST NATIVES.

BUT AFTER THE *BRIDGE WAR OF 1836* (LONG STORY), ROCKEFELLER TURNED THE FLATS INTO AN INDUSTRIAL POWERHOUSE.

BANKRUPTCY EVENTUALLY FORCED BUSINESSES TO PULL OUT, LEAVING BEHIND THE KIND OF ABANDONED WAREHOUSES ANY GOOD SUPER-VILLAIN WOULD BE PROUD TO CALL *HOME.*

THINGS TURNED AROUND FOR A BIT WHEN I WAS IN HIGH SCHOOL, AS THE FLATS BECAME THE DENSEST COLLECTION OF *BARS* AND *RESTAURANTS* IN THE ENTIRE *RUST BELT.*

BUT A BUNCH OF DROWNING DEATHS IN 2000, COMBINED WITH ALL SORTS OF FIRE CODE VIOLATIONS, HELPED *SHUT DOWN* MOST OF THE BEST JOINTS.

STILL, THE BEER IS CHEAP OUT HERE (AND RARELY FLAT), SO WE MAKE DO.

OKAY, EVERYTHING'S IN TO OUR QUEBECOR REP, AND OUR FIRST SOLICIT WILL BE OUT NEXT MONTH, SO I THINK IT'S TIME FOR *PHASE ONE*.

ALREADY?

I THOUGHT WE WERE GONNA SAVE OUR BIG PUBLICITY STUNT FOR THE WEEK THE BOOK'S SUPPOSED TO DROP.

CASE, WE'RE GOING TO BE COMPETING AGAINST *HUNDREDS* OF NEW COMICS, AND OURS STARS A CHARACTER WHO'S BEEN OUT OF PRINT FOR *DECADES*.

WE'VE GOT TO GET THE HYPE MACHINE ROLLING *NOW*, AND WE NEED SOMETHING THAT WILL MAKE US STAND OUT FROM THE PACK.

JOE KAVALIER AND SAM CLAY WERE AS INNOVATIVE WITH THEIR *MARKETING* AS THEY WERE WITH THEIR ART.

I MEAN, THEY HAD THE ESCAPIST PUNCHING *HITLER* ON THEIR FIRST COVER, BACK WHEN SOMETHING LIKE THAT WAS UNHEARD OF.

WE'RE NOT GONNA PUT *OSAMA* IN OUR BOOK, ARE WE?

SO WE'RE GONNA HAVE DENNY DRESS UP IN YOUR ANTIQUE ESCAPIST COSTUME--AND *WHAT?* HAND OUT FREE COPIES OF ISSUE #1 AT THE MALL?

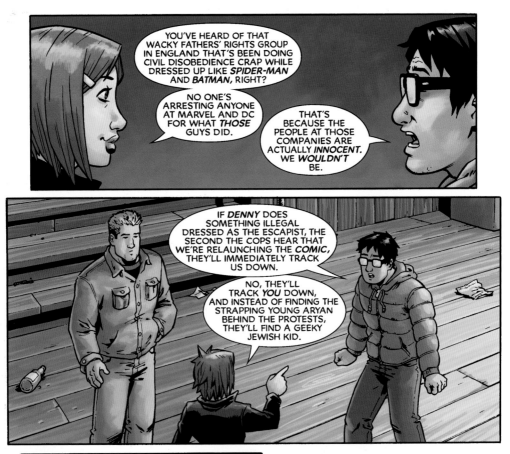

YOU'VE HEARD OF THAT WACKY FATHERS' RIGHTS GROUP IN ENGLAND THAT'S BEEN DOING CIVIL DISOBEDIENCE CRAP WHILE DRESSED UP LIKE *SPIDER-MAN* AND *BATMAN,* RIGHT?

NO ONE'S ARRESTING ANYONE AT MARVEL AND DC FOR WHAT *THOSE* GUYS DID.

THAT'S BECAUSE THE PEOPLE AT THOSE COMPANIES ARE ACTUALLY *INNOCENT.* WE *WOULDN'T* BE.

IF *DENNY* DOES SOMETHING ILLEGAL DRESSED AS THE ESCAPIST, THE SECOND THE COPS HEAR THAT WE'RE RELAUNCHING THE *COMIC,* THEY'LL IMMEDIATELY TRACK US DOWN.

NO, THEY'LL TRACK *YOU* DOWN, AND INSTEAD OF FINDING THE STRAPPING YOUNG ARYAN BEHIND THE PROTESTS, THEY'LL FIND A GEEKY JEWISH KID.

I'M NOT ARYAN, I'M *DUTCH.*

AND I'M NOT A *GEEK!*

PROVE IT.

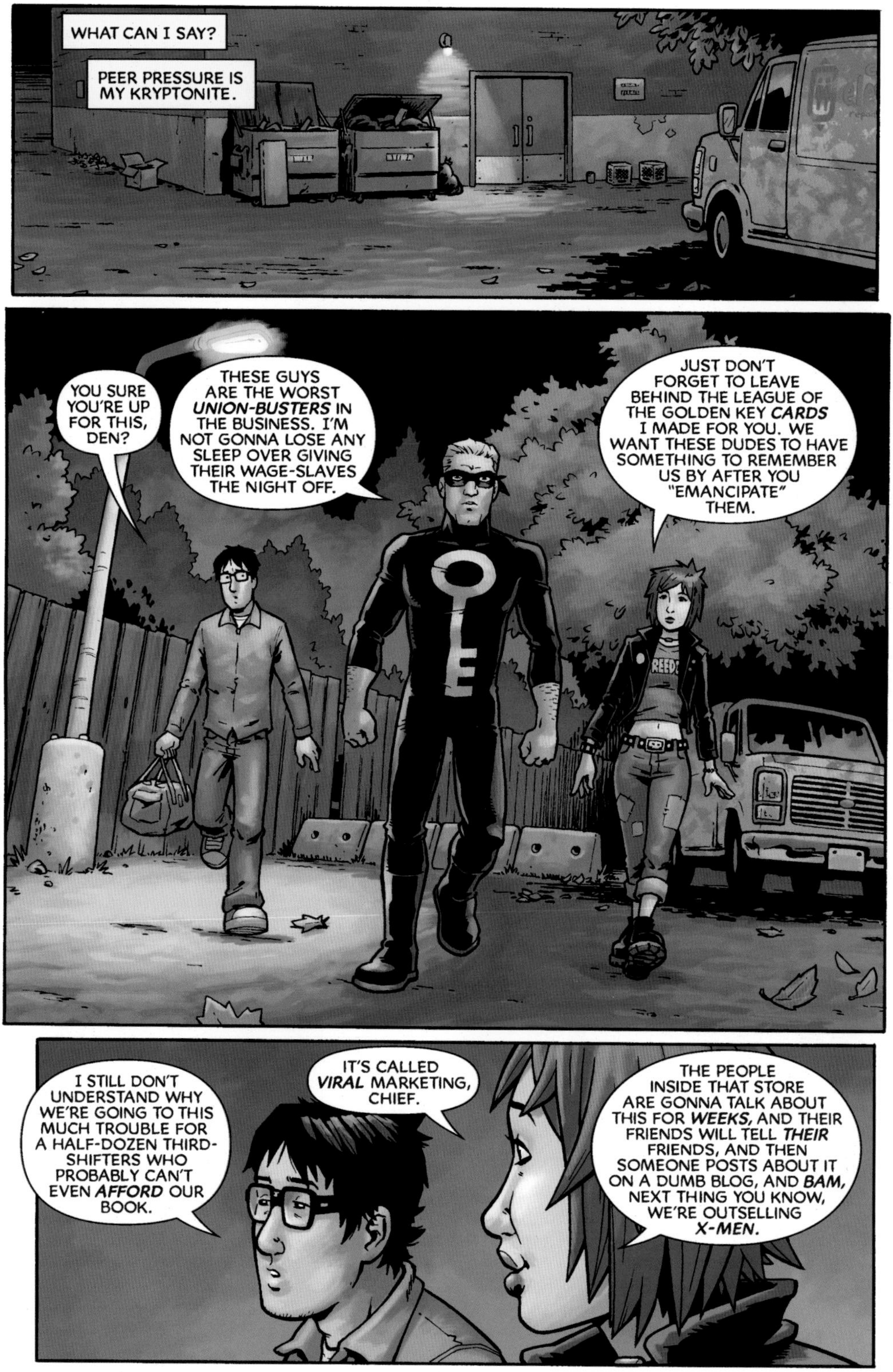
WHAT CAN I SAY?
PEER PRESSURE IS MY KRYPTONITE.
YOU SURE YOU'RE UP FOR THIS, DEN?
THESE GUYS ARE THE WORST *UNION-BUSTERS* IN THE BUSINESS. I'M NOT GONNA LOSE ANY SLEEP OVER GIVING THEIR WAGE-SLAVES THE NIGHT OFF.
JUST DON'T FORGET TO LEAVE BEHIND THE GOLDEN KEY *CARDS* I MADE FOR YOU. WE WANT THESE DUDES TO HAVE SOMETHING TO REMEMBER US BY AFTER YOU "EMANCIPATE" THEM.
I STILL DON'T UNDERSTAND WHY WE'RE GOING TO THIS MUCH TROUBLE FOR A HALF-DOZEN THIRD-SHIFTERS WHO PROBABLY CAN'T EVEN *AFFORD* OUR BOOK.
IT'S CALLED *VIRAL* MARKETING, CHIEF.
THE PEOPLE INSIDE THAT STORE ARE GONNA TALK ABOUT THIS FOR *WEEKS,* AND THEIR FRIENDS WILL TELL *THEIR* FRIENDS, AND THEN SOMEONE POSTS ABOUT IT ON A DUMB BLOG, AND *BAM,* NEXT THING YOU KNOW, WE'RE OUTSELLING *X-MEN.*

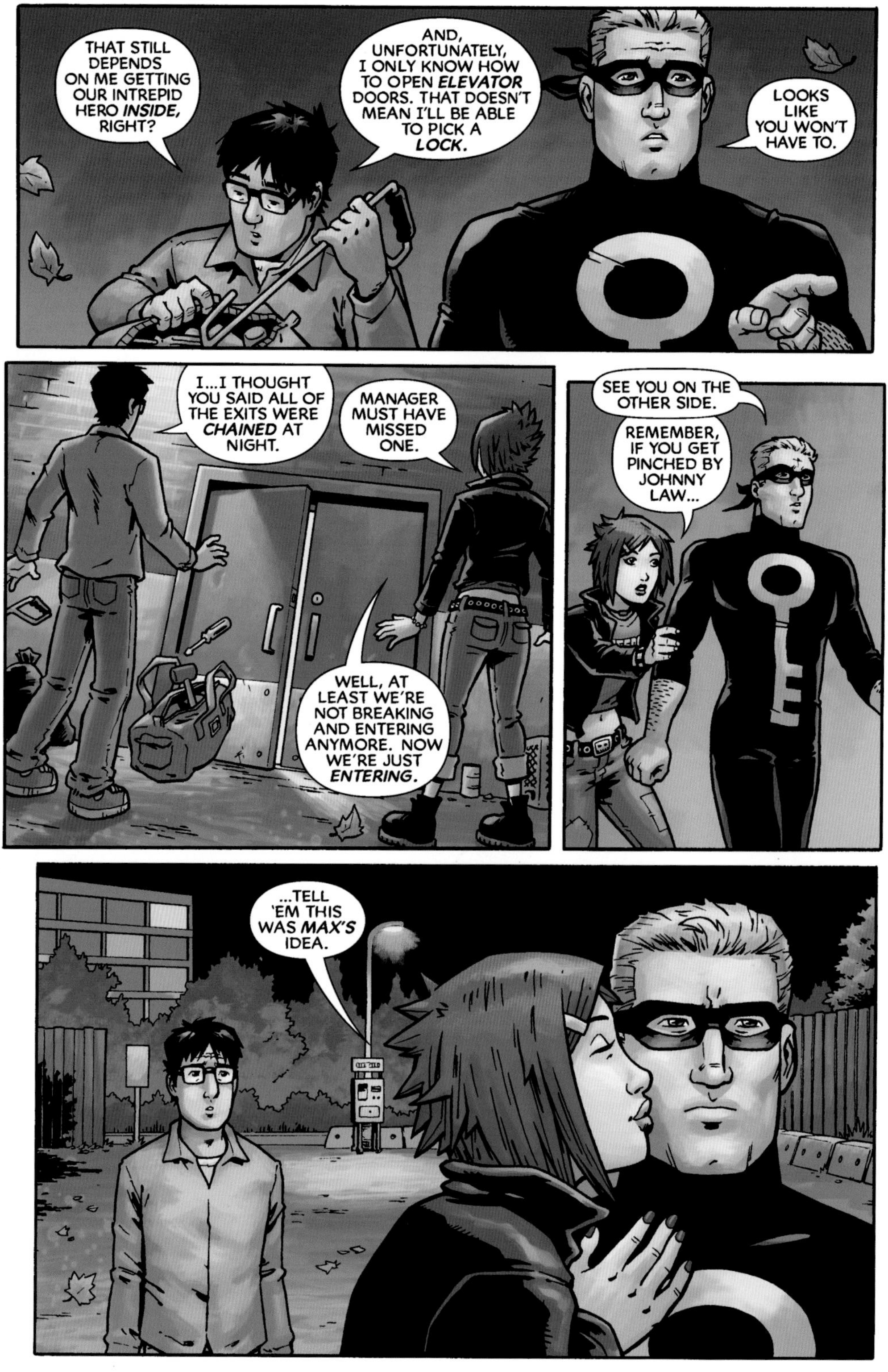
THAT STILL DEPENDS ON ME GETTING OUR INTREPID HERO *INSIDE,* RIGHT?
AND, UNFORTUNATELY, I ONLY KNOW HOW TO OPEN *ELEVATOR* DOORS. THAT DOESN'T MEAN I'LL BE ABLE TO PICK A *LOCK*.
LOOKS LIKE YOU WON'T HAVE TO.
I...I THOUGHT YOU SAID ALL OF THE EXITS WERE *CHAINED* AT NIGHT.
MANAGER MUST HAVE MISSED ONE.
WELL, AT LEAST WE'RE NOT BREAKING AND ENTERING ANYMORE. NOW WE'RE JUST *ENTERING.*
SEE YOU ON THE OTHER SIDE.
REMEMBER, IF YOU GET PINCHED BY JOHNNY LAW...
...TELL 'EM THIS WAS *MAX'S* IDEA.

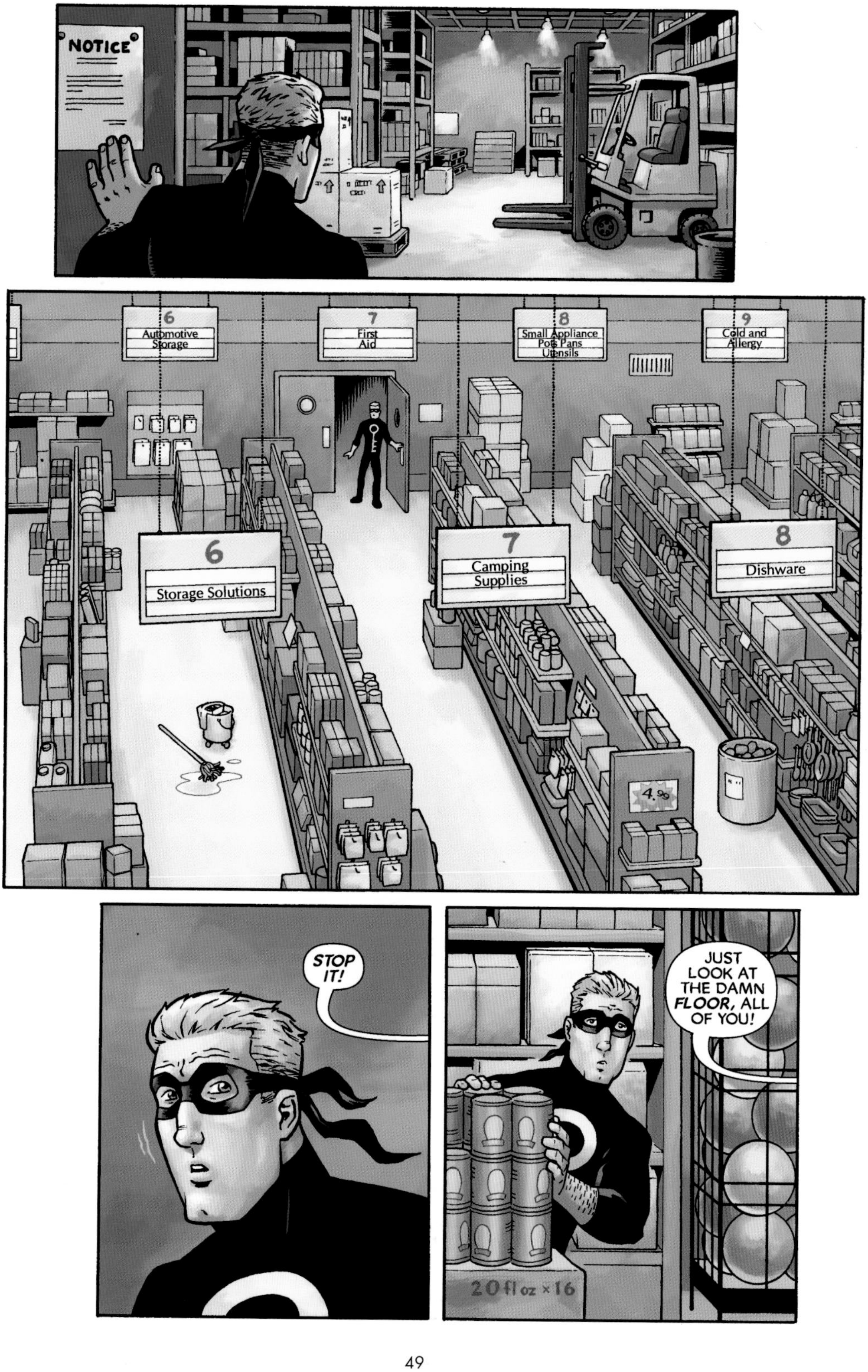
NOTICE
6 Automotive Storage
7 First Aid
8 Small Appliance Pots Pans Utensils
9 Cold and Allergy
6 Storage Solutions
7 Camping Supplies
8 Dishware
STOP IT!
JUST LOOK AT THE DAMN *FLOOR,* ALL OF YOU!
20 fl oz ×16

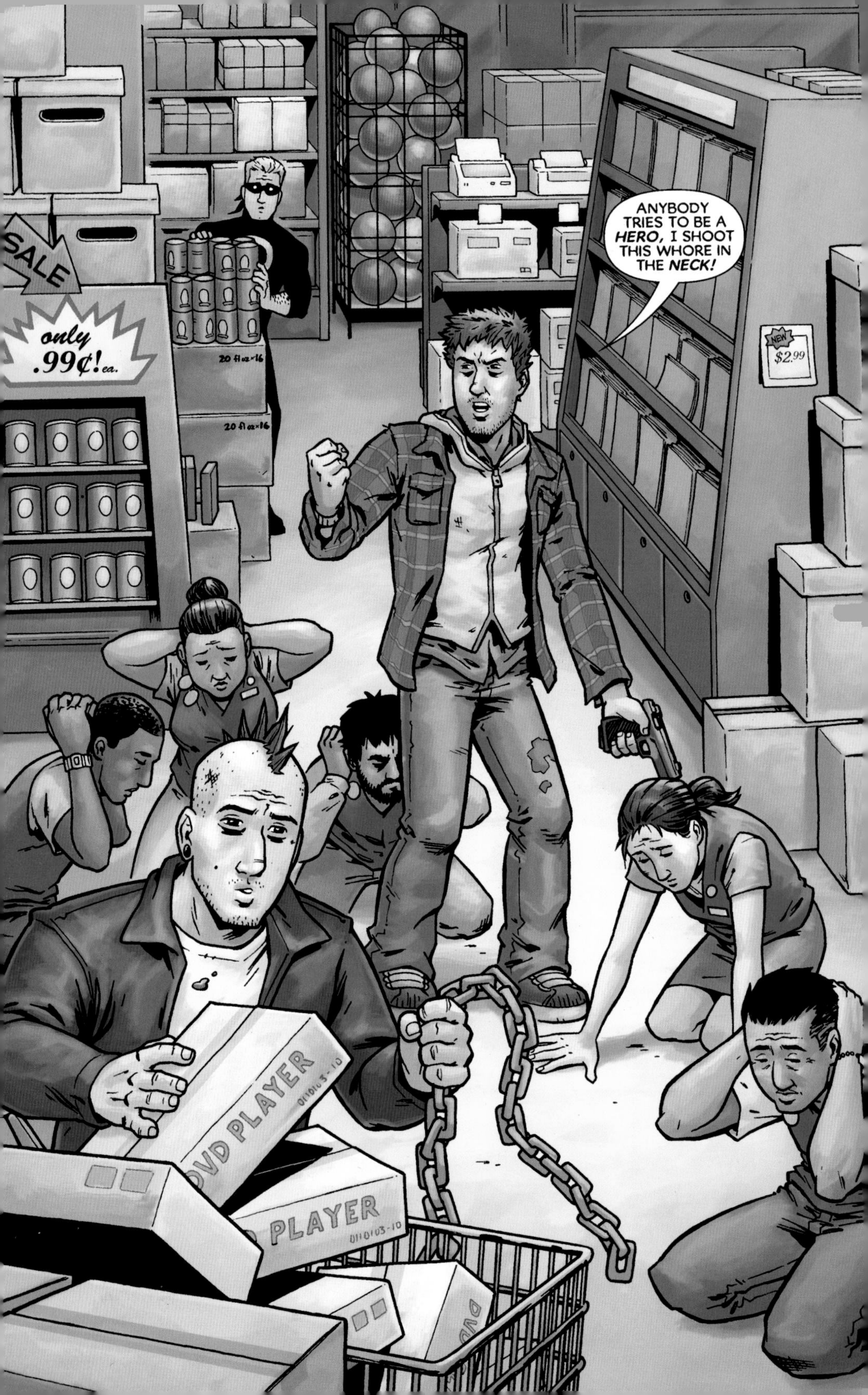
SALE
only .99¢! ea.
20 fl oz-16
20 fl oz-16
NEW $2.99
ANYBODY TRIES TO BE A *HERO,* I SHOOT THIS WHORE IN THE *NECK!*
DVD PLAYER
PLAYER

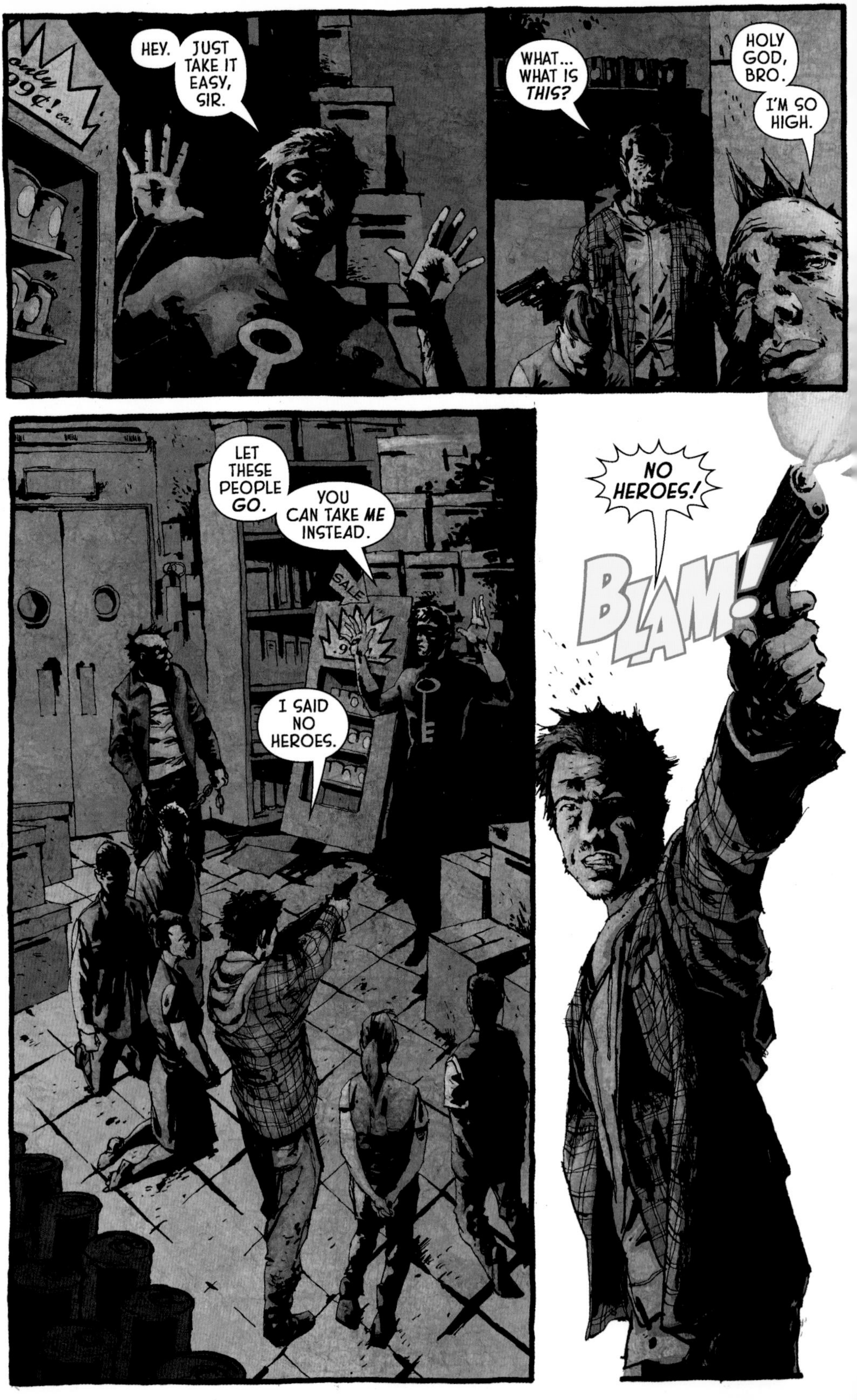
HEY.
JUST TAKE IT EASY, SIR.
WHAT... WHAT IS THIS?
HOLY GOD, BRO.
I'M SO HIGH.
LET THESE PEOPLE GO.
YOU CAN TAKE ME INSTEAD.
I SAID NO HEROES.
NO HEROES!
BLAM!

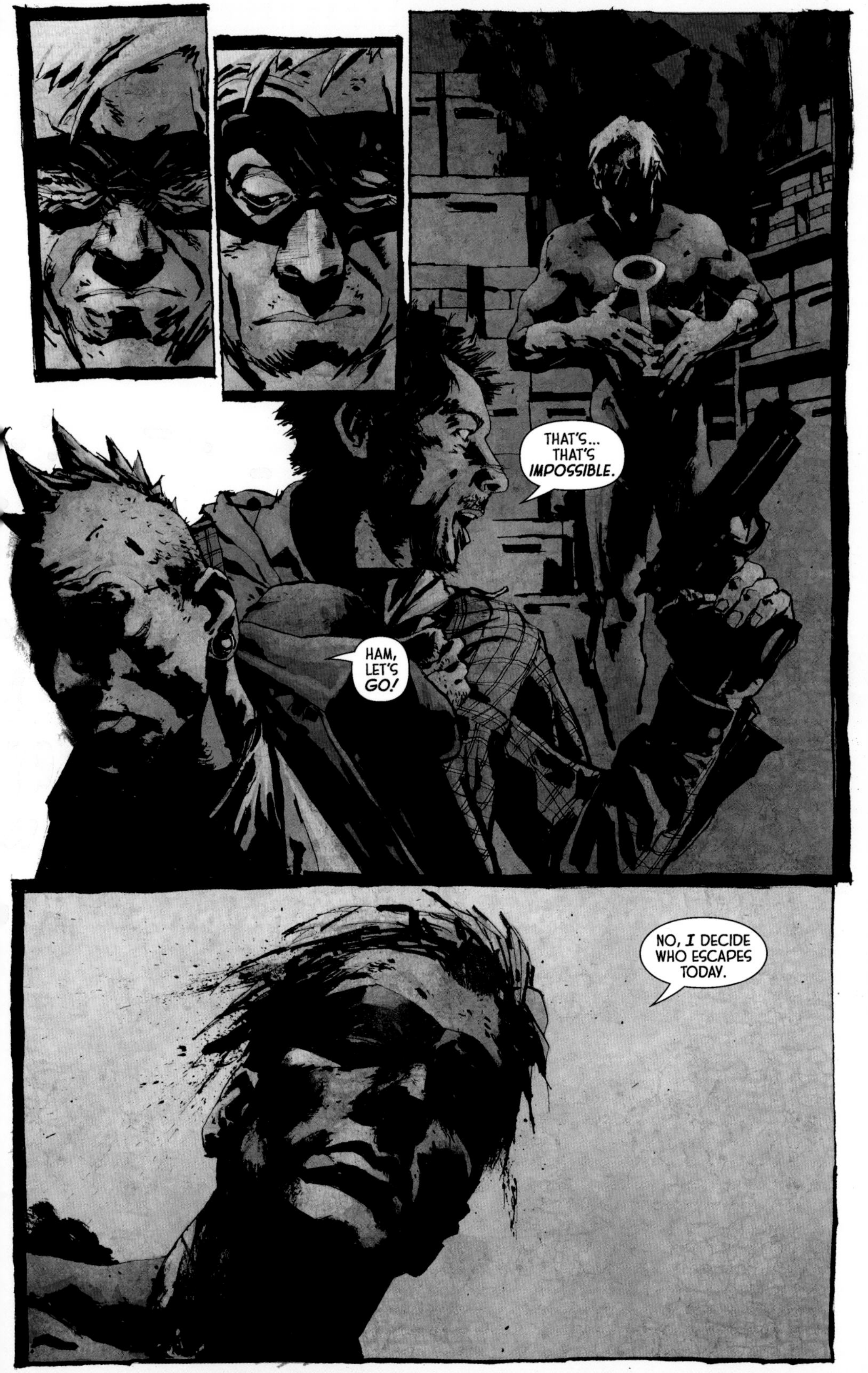

THAT'S... THAT'S *IMPOSSIBLE.*
HAM, LET'S *GO!*
NO, *I* DECIDE WHO ESCAPES TODAY.

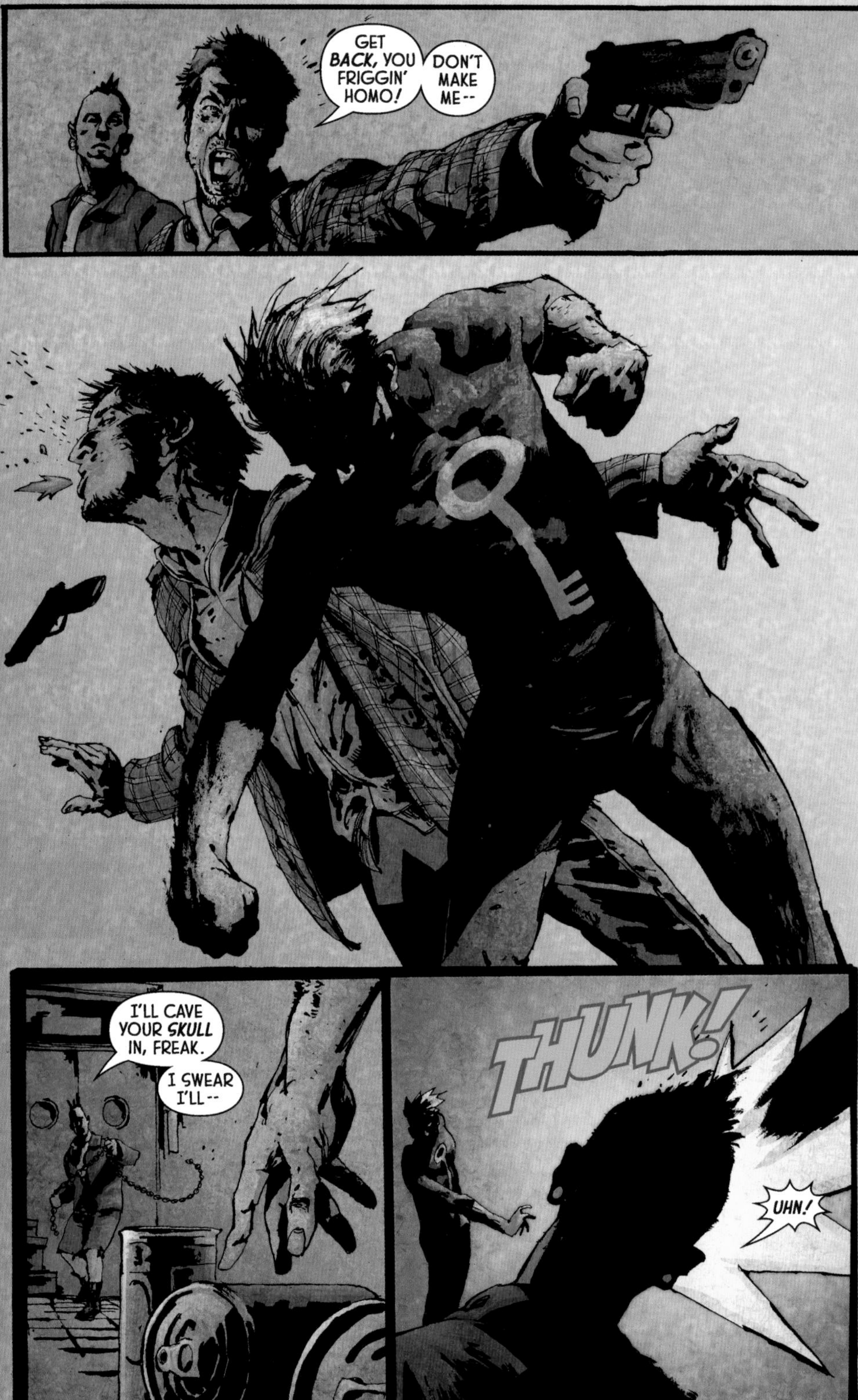
GET BACK, YOU FRIGGIN' HOMO!
DON'T MAKE ME--
I'LL CAVE YOUR SKULL IN, FREAK.
I SWEAR I'LL--
THUNK!
UHN!

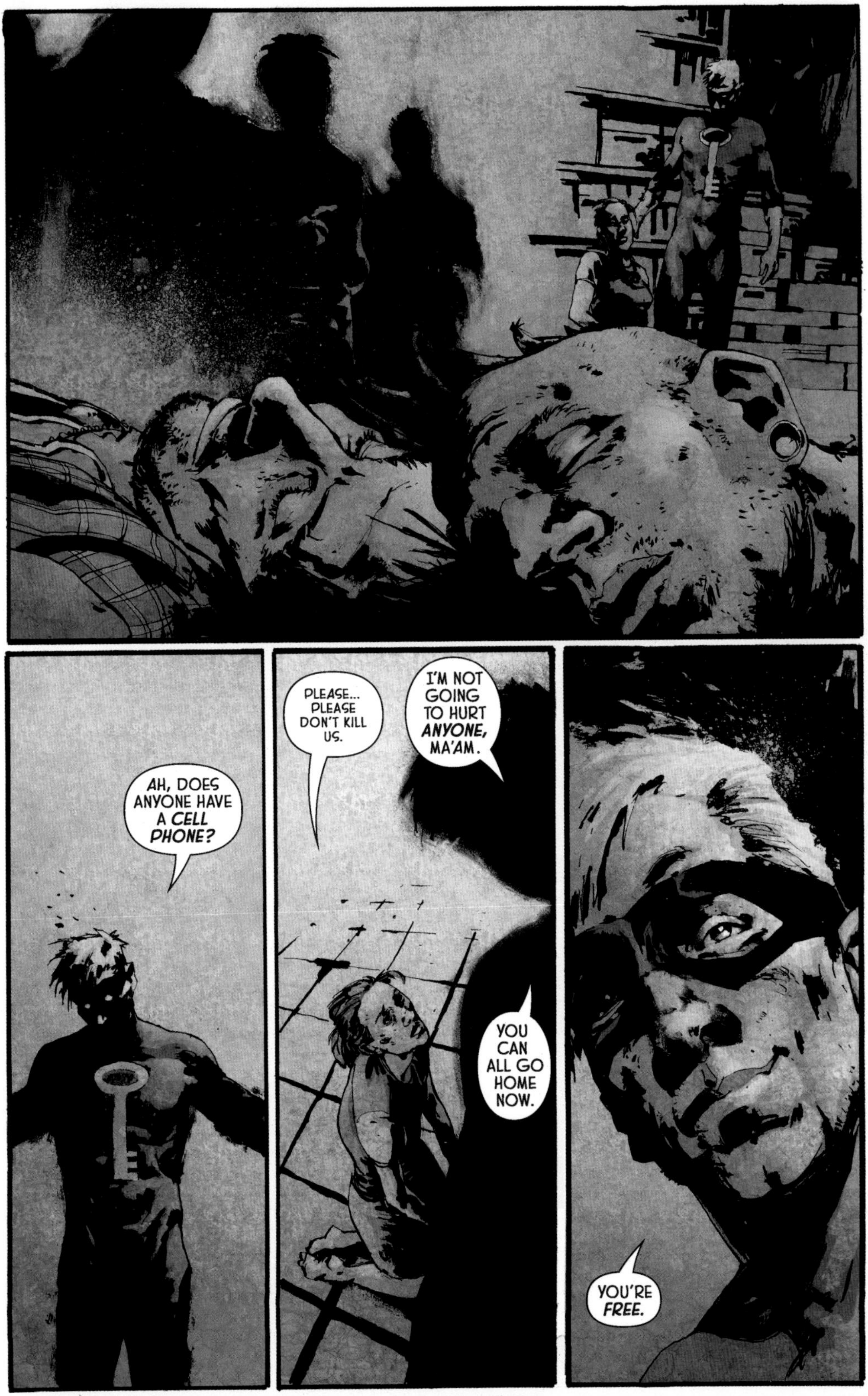
AH, DOES ANYONE HAVE A *CELL PHONE?*
PLEASE... PLEASE DON'T KILL US.
I'M NOT GOING TO HURT *ANYONE,* MA'AM.
YOU CAN ALL GO HOME NOW.
YOU'RE *FREE.*

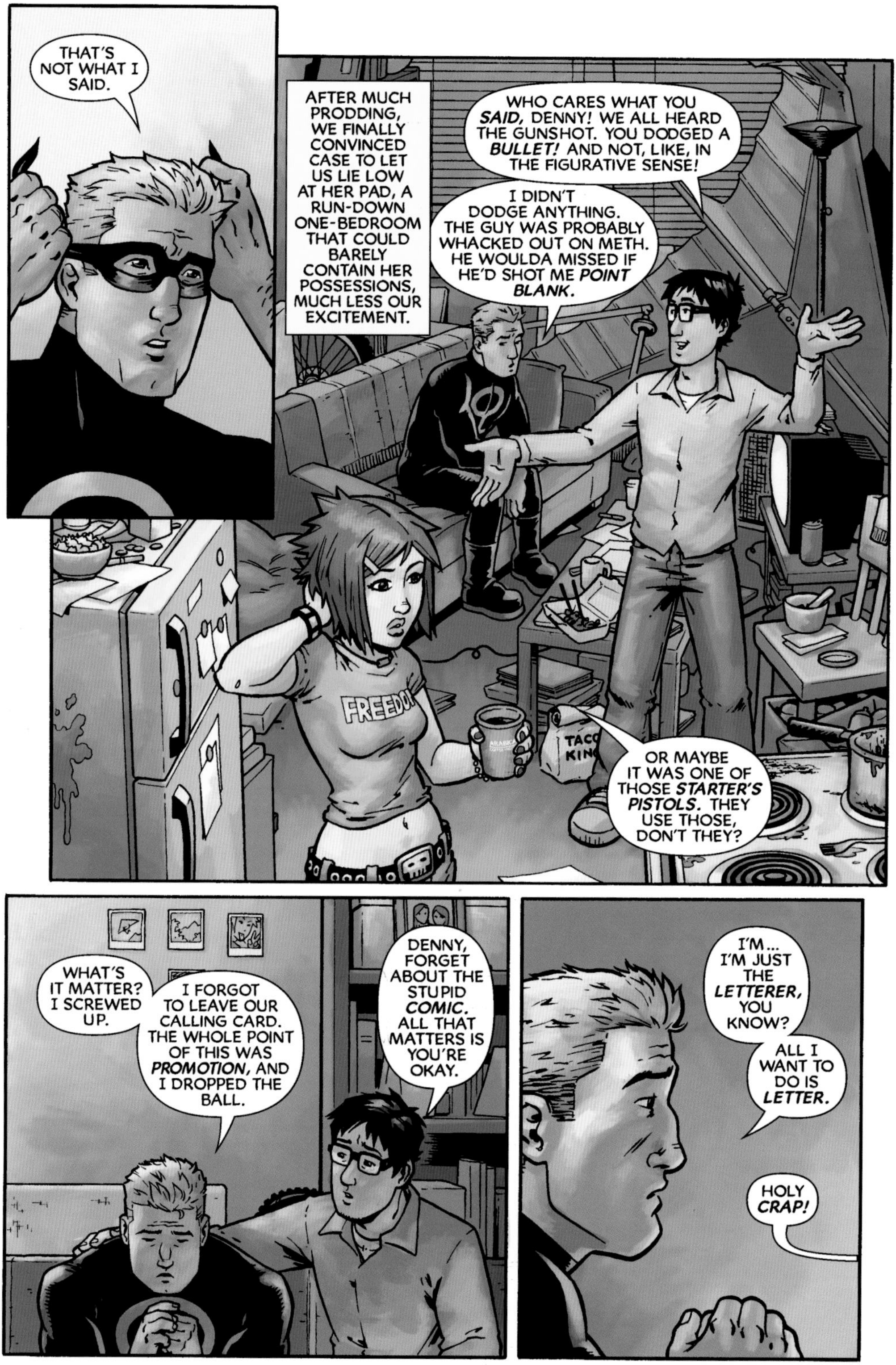
THAT'S NOT WHAT I SAID.
AFTER MUCH PRODDING, WE FINALLY CONVINCED CASE TO LET US LIE LOW AT HER PAD, A RUN-DOWN ONE-BEDROOM THAT COULD BARELY CONTAIN HER POSSESSIONS, MUCH LESS OUR EXCITEMENT.
WHO CARES WHAT YOU *SAID,* DENNY! WE ALL HEARD THE GUNSHOT. YOU DODGED A *BULLET!* AND NOT, LIKE, IN THE FIGURATIVE SENSE!
I DIDN'T DODGE ANYTHING. THE GUY WAS PROBABLY WHACKED OUT ON METH. HE WOULDA MISSED IF HE'D SHOT ME *POINT BLANK.*
FREEDO
TACO KING
OR MAYBE IT WAS ONE OF THOSE *STARTER'S PISTOLS.* THEY USE THOSE, DON'T THEY?
WHAT'S IT MATTER? I SCREWED UP.
I FORGOT TO LEAVE OUR CALLING CARD. THE WHOLE POINT OF THIS WAS *PROMOTION,* AND I DROPPED THE BALL.
DENNY, FORGET ABOUT THE STUPID *COMIC.* ALL THAT MATTERS IS YOU'RE OKAY.
I'M... I'M JUST THE *LETTERER,* YOU KNOW?
ALL I WANT TO DO IS *LETTER.*
HOLY *CRAP!*

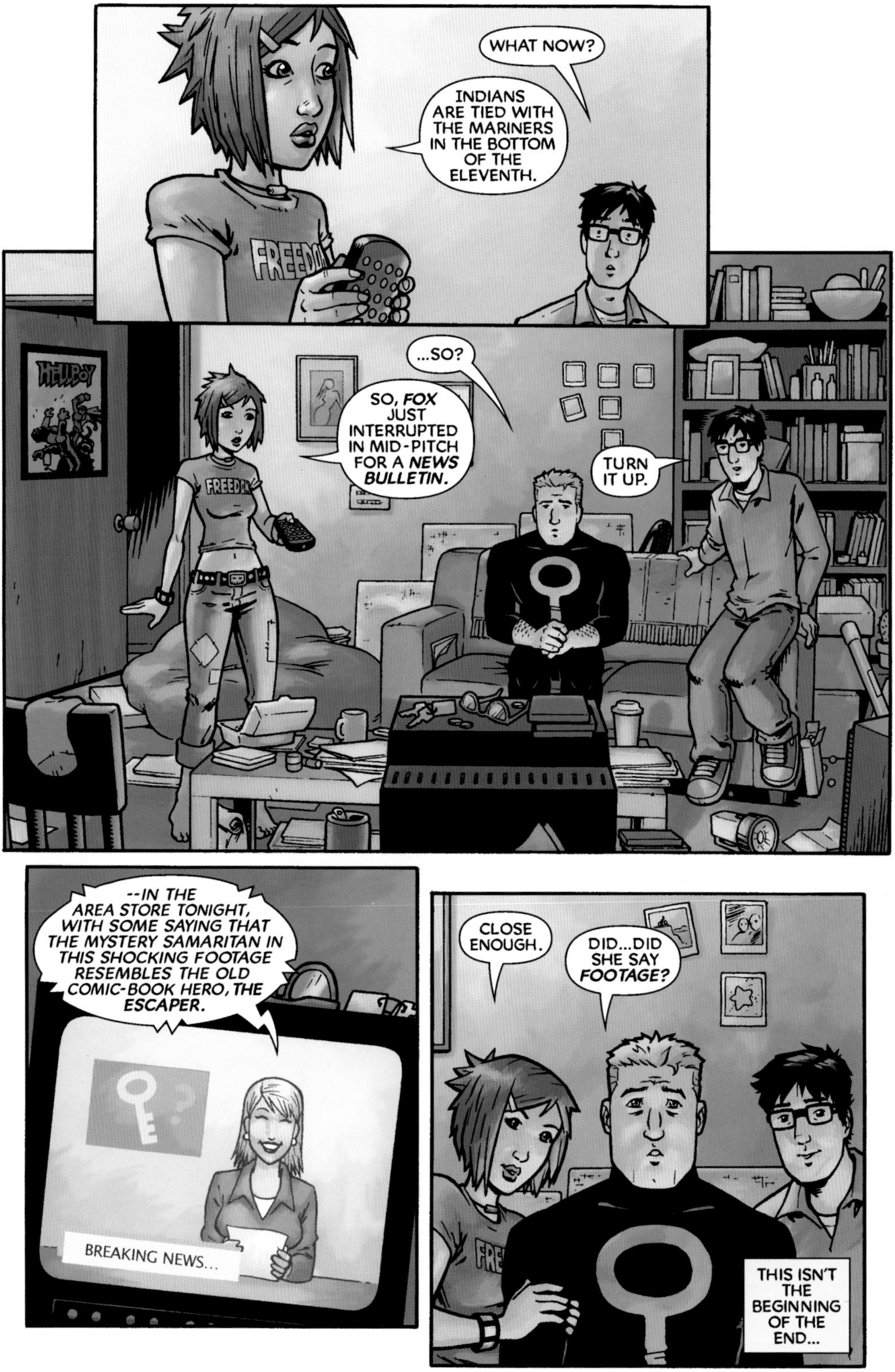
WHAT NOW?
INDIANS ARE TIED WITH THE MARINERS IN THE BOTTOM OF THE ELEVENTH.
FREEDOM
...SO?
SO, *FOX* JUST INTERRUPTED IN MID-PITCH FOR A *NEWS BULLETIN.*
TURN IT UP.
HELLBOY
--IN THE AREA STORE TONIGHT, WITH SOME SAYING THAT THE MYSTERY SAMARITAN IN THIS SHOCKING FOOTAGE RESEMBLES THE OLD COMIC-BOOK HERO, THE ESCAPER.
BREAKING NEWS...
CLOSE ENOUGH.
DID...DID SHE SAY *FOOTAGE?*
THIS ISN'T THE BEGINNING OF THE END...

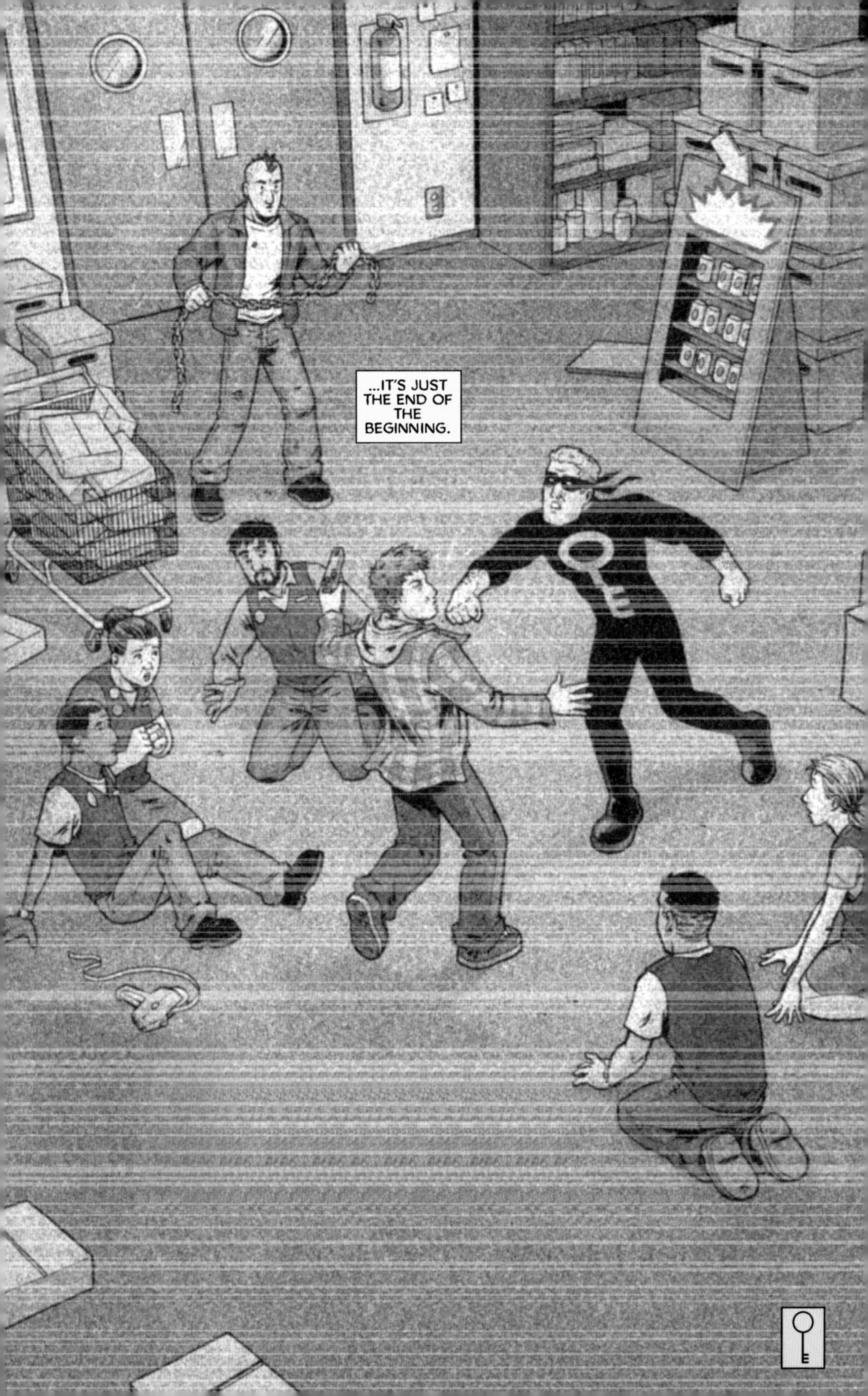
...IT'S JUST THE END OF THE BEGINNING.

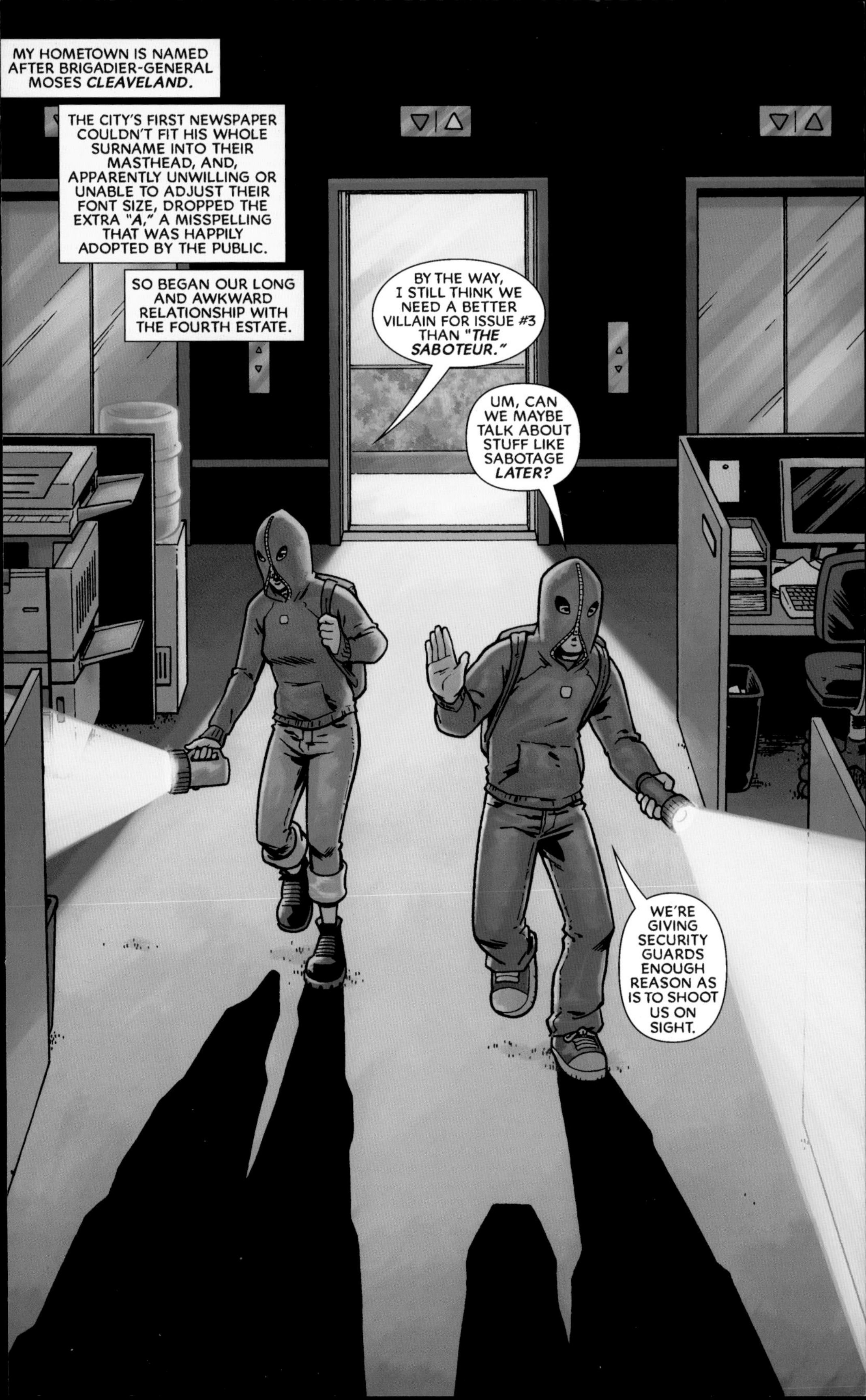
MY HOMETOWN IS NAMED AFTER BRIGADIER-GENERAL MOSES *CLEAVELAND*.
THE CITY'S FIRST NEWSPAPER COULDN'T FIT HIS WHOLE SURNAME INTO THEIR MASTHEAD, AND, APPARENTLY UNWILLING OR UNABLE TO ADJUST THEIR FONT SIZE, DROPPED THE EXTRA "*A*," A MISSPELLING THAT WAS HAPPILY ADOPTED BY THE PUBLIC.
SO BEGAN OUR LONG AND AWKWARD RELATIONSHIP WITH THE FOURTH ESTATE.
BY THE WAY, I STILL THINK WE NEED A BETTER VILLAIN FOR ISSUE #3 THAN "*THE SABOTEUR*."
UM, CAN WE MAYBE TALK ABOUT STUFF LIKE SABOTAGE *LATER?*
WE'RE GIVING SECURITY GUARDS ENOUGH REASON AS IS TO SHOOT US ON SIGHT.

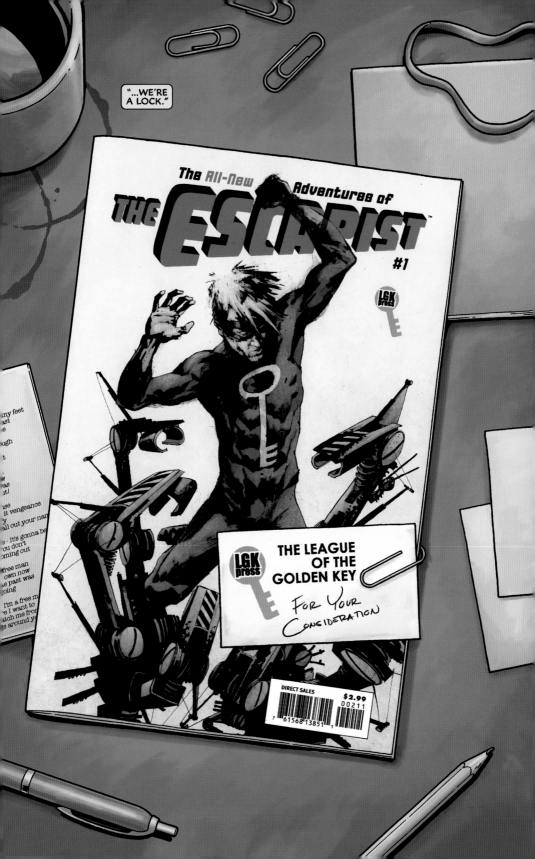

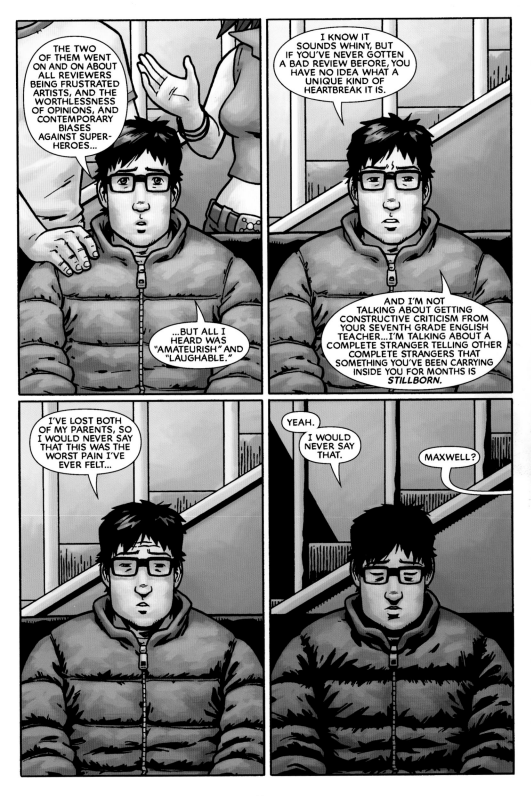

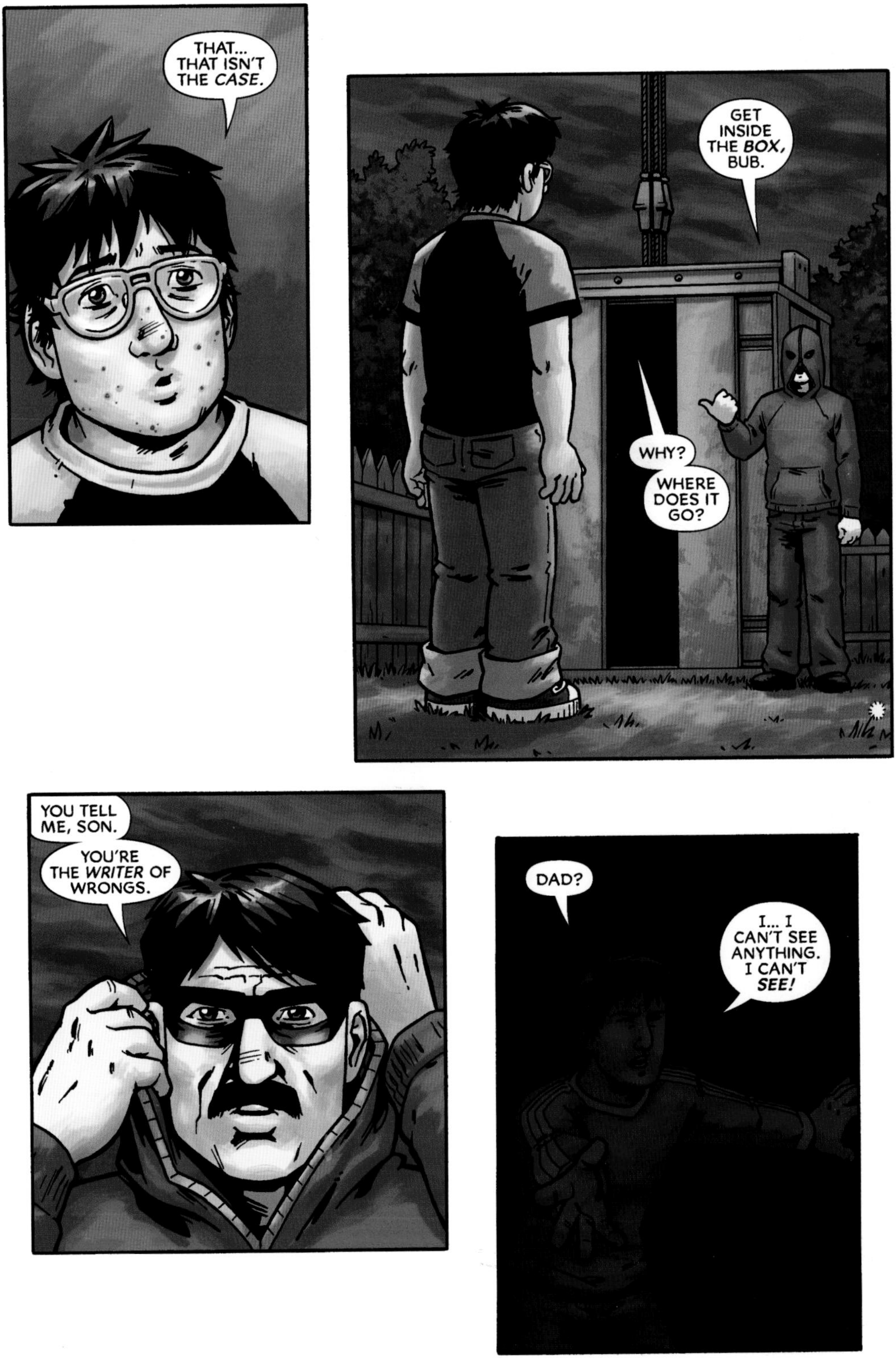
THAT... THAT ISN'T THE *CASE.*
GET INSIDE THE *BOX,* BUB.
WHY?
WHERE DOES IT GO?
YOU TELL ME, SON.
YOU'RE THE *WRITER* OF WRONGS.
DAD?
I... I CAN'T SEE ANYTHING. I CAN'T *SEE!*

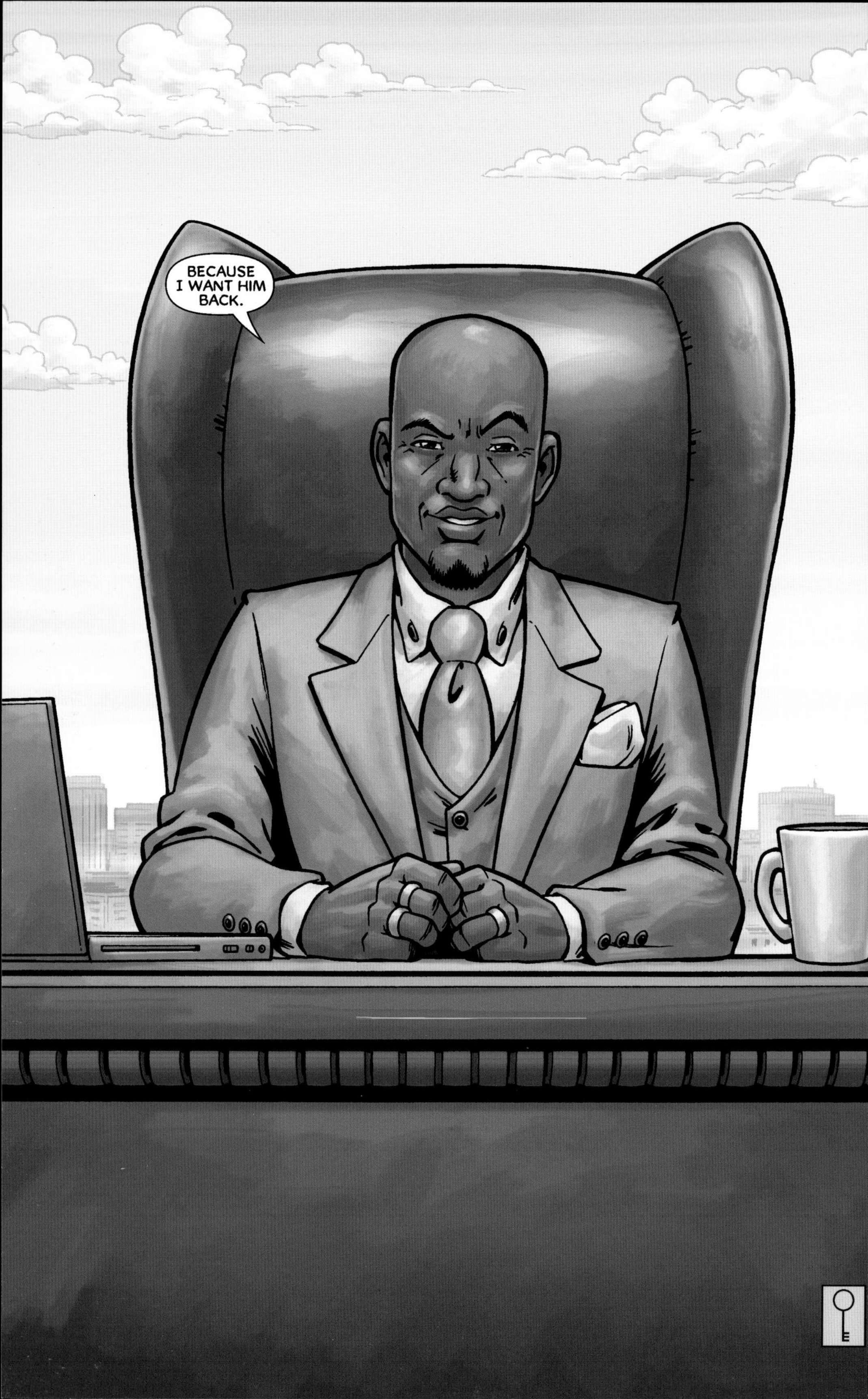
BECAUSE I WANT HIM BACK.

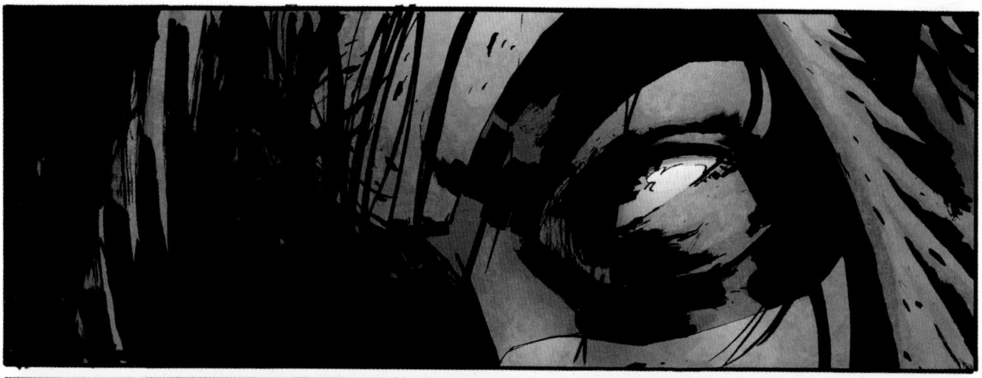

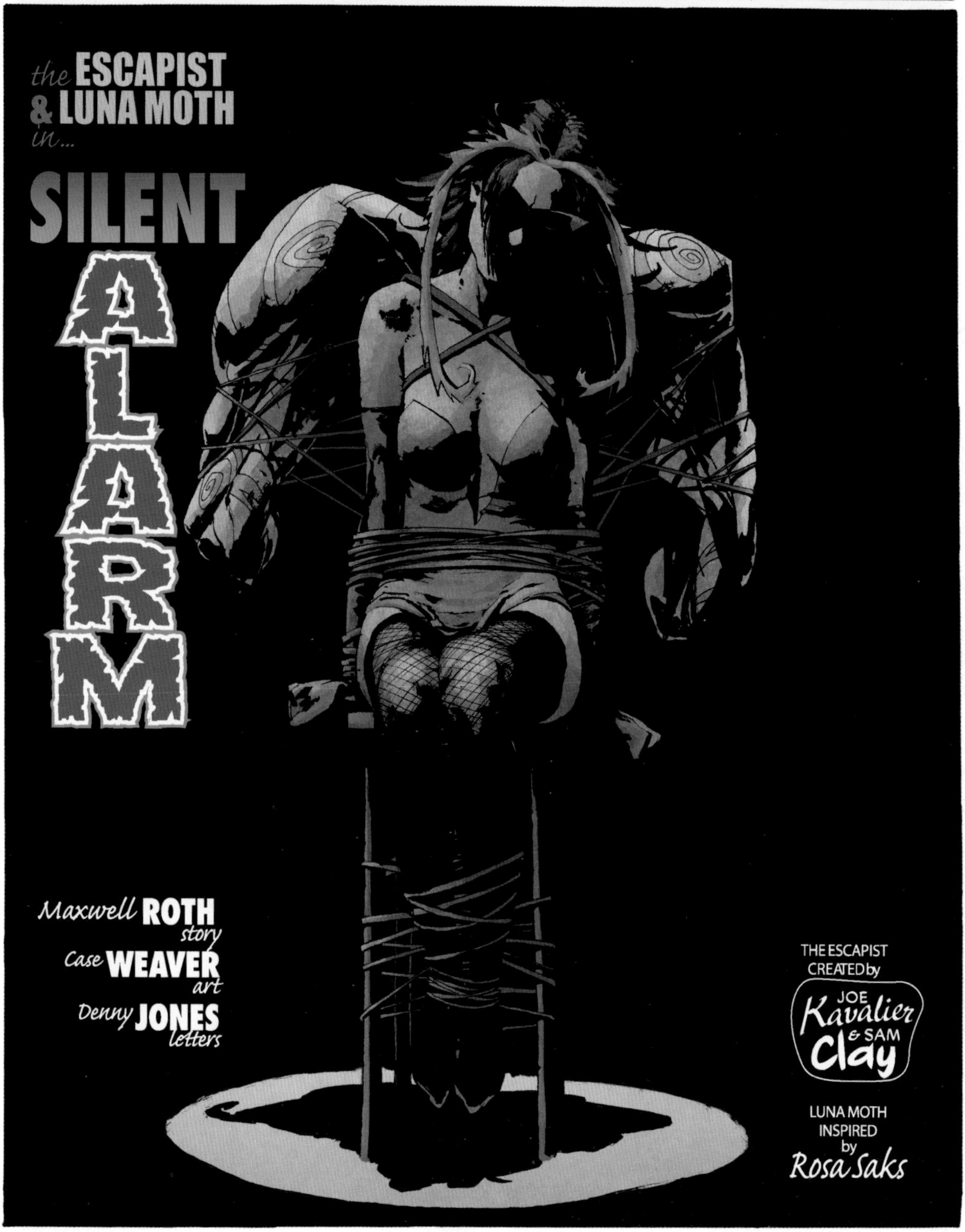
the ESCAPIST
& LUNA MOTH
in...
SILENT
ALARM
Maxwell ROTH
story
Case WEAVER
art
Denny JONES
letters
THE ESCAPIST
CREATED by
JOE Kavalier & SAM Clay
LUNA MOTH
INSPIRED
by
Rosa Saks

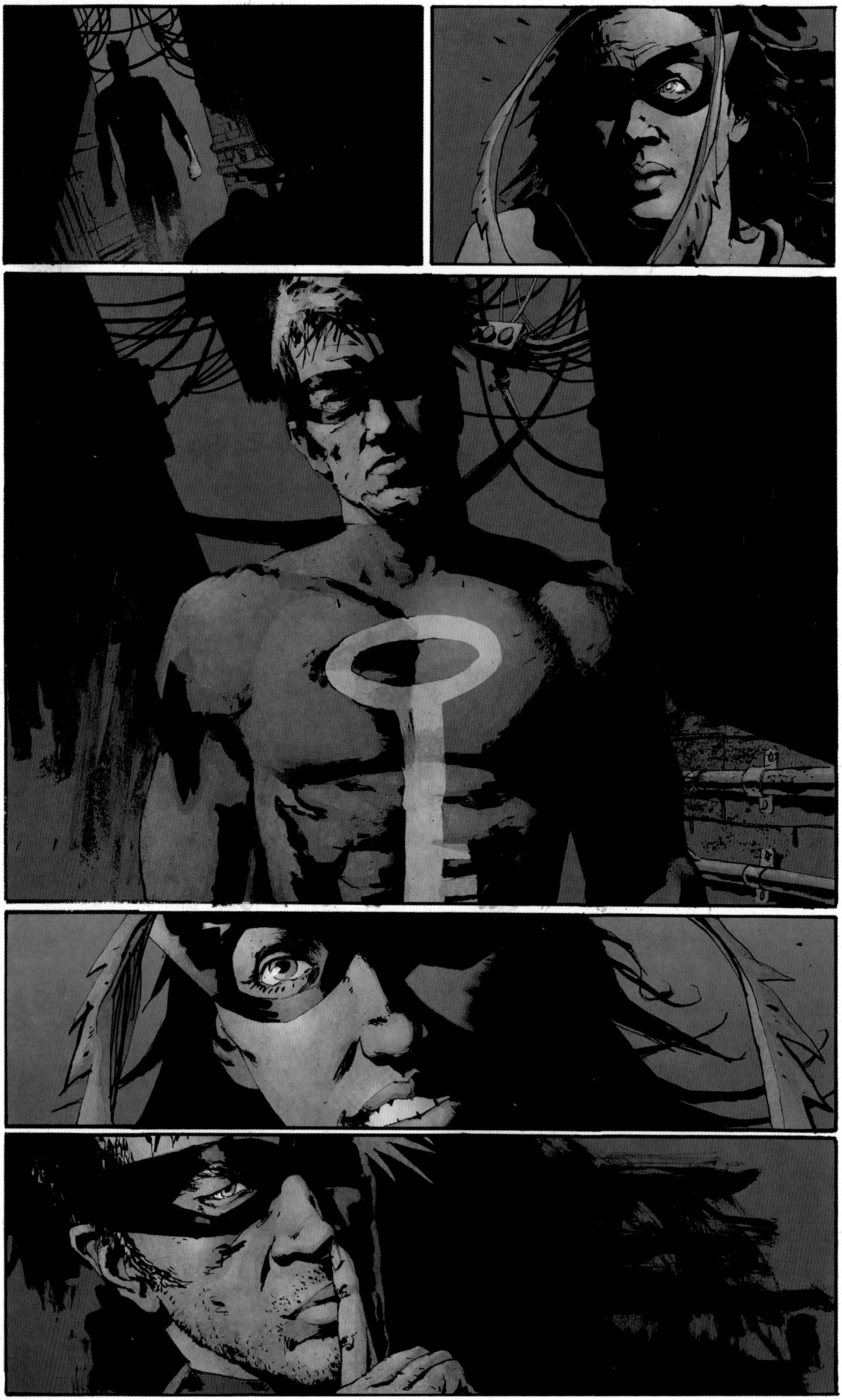

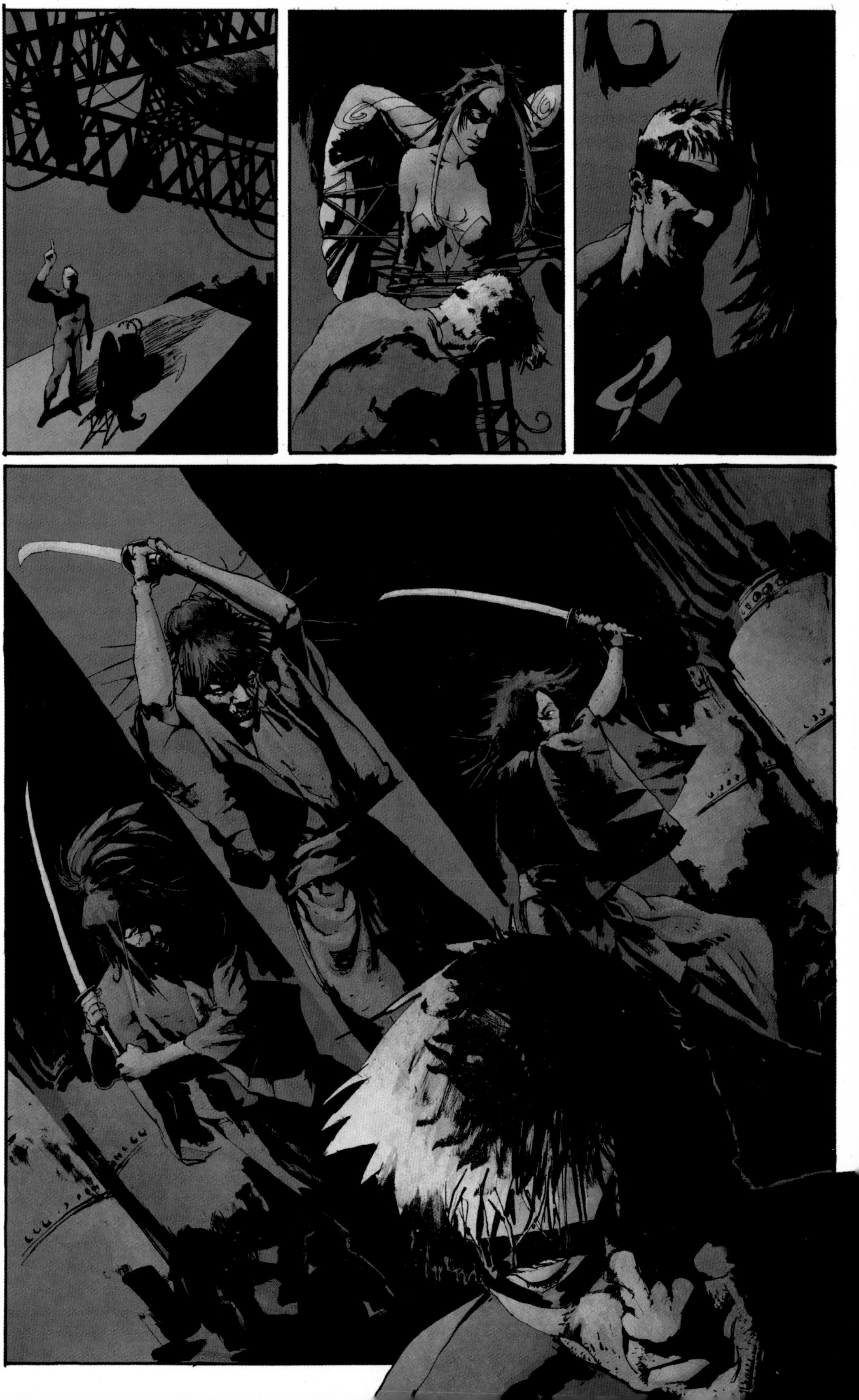

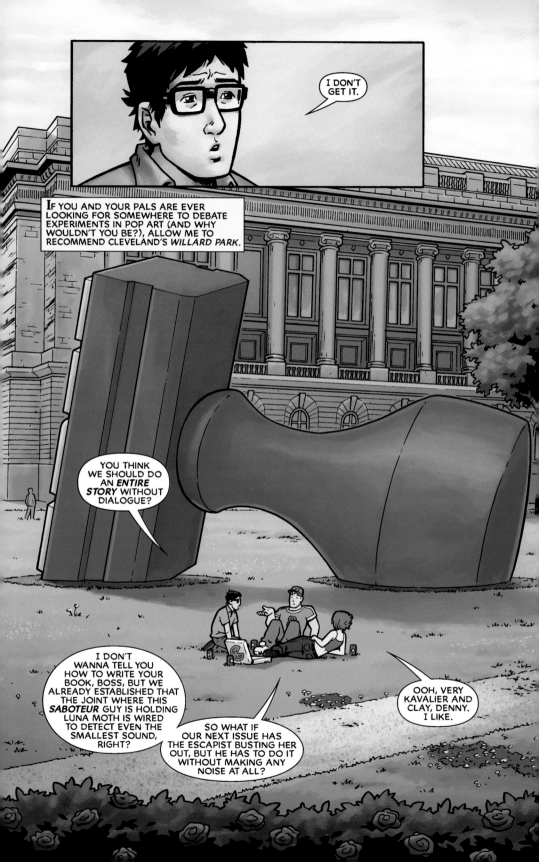

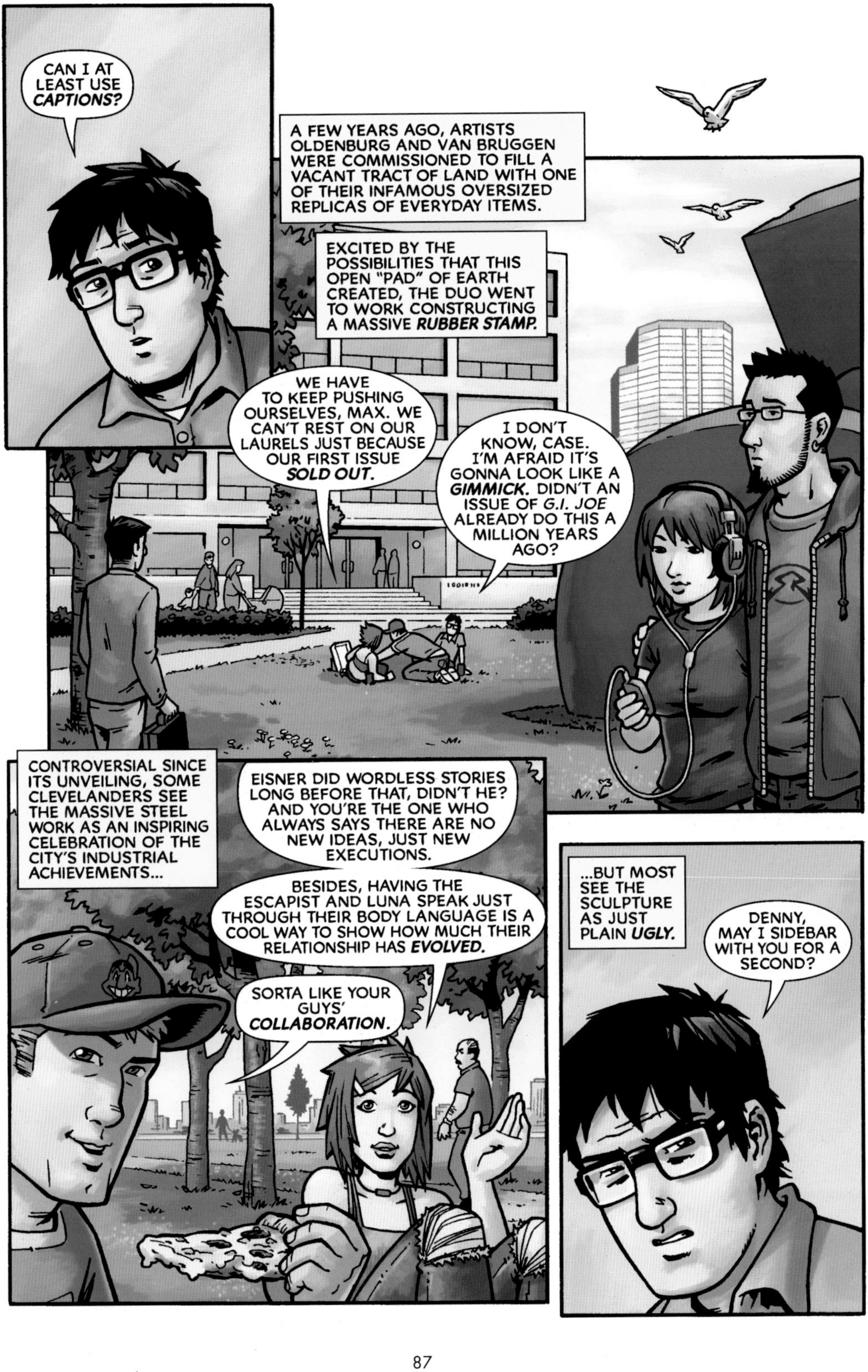
CAN I AT LEAST USE *CAPTIONS?*
A FEW YEARS AGO, ARTISTS OLDENBURG AND VAN BRUGGEN WERE COMMISSIONED TO FILL A VACANT TRACT OF LAND WITH ONE OF THEIR INFAMOUS OVERSIZED REPLICAS OF EVERYDAY ITEMS.
EXCITED BY THE POSSIBILITIES THAT THIS OPEN "PAD" OF EARTH CREATED, THE DUO WENT TO WORK CONSTRUCTING A MASSIVE *RUBBER STAMP.*
WE HAVE TO KEEP PUSHING OURSELVES, MAX. WE CAN'T REST ON OUR LAURELS JUST BECAUSE OUR FIRST ISSUE *SOLD OUT*.
I DON'T KNOW, CASE. I'M AFRAID IT'S GONNA LOOK LIKE A *GIMMICK.* DIDN'T AN ISSUE OF *G.I. JOE* ALREADY DO THIS A MILLION YEARS AGO?
CONTROVERSIAL SINCE ITS UNVEILING, SOME CLEVELANDERS SEE THE MASSIVE STEEL WORK AS AN INSPIRING CELEBRATION OF THE CITY'S INDUSTRIAL ACHIEVEMENTS...
EISNER DID WORDLESS STORIES LONG BEFORE THAT, DIDN'T HE? AND YOU'RE THE ONE WHO ALWAYS SAYS THERE ARE NO NEW IDEAS, JUST NEW EXECUTIONS.
BESIDES, HAVING THE ESCAPIST AND LUNA SPEAK JUST THROUGH THEIR BODY LANGUAGE IS A COOL WAY TO SHOW HOW MUCH THEIR RELATIONSHIP HAS *EVOLVED.*
SORTA LIKE YOUR GUYS' *COLLABORATION*.
...BUT MOST SEE THE SCULPTURE AS JUST PLAIN *UGLY.*
DENNY, MAY I SIDEBAR WITH YOU FOR A SECOND?

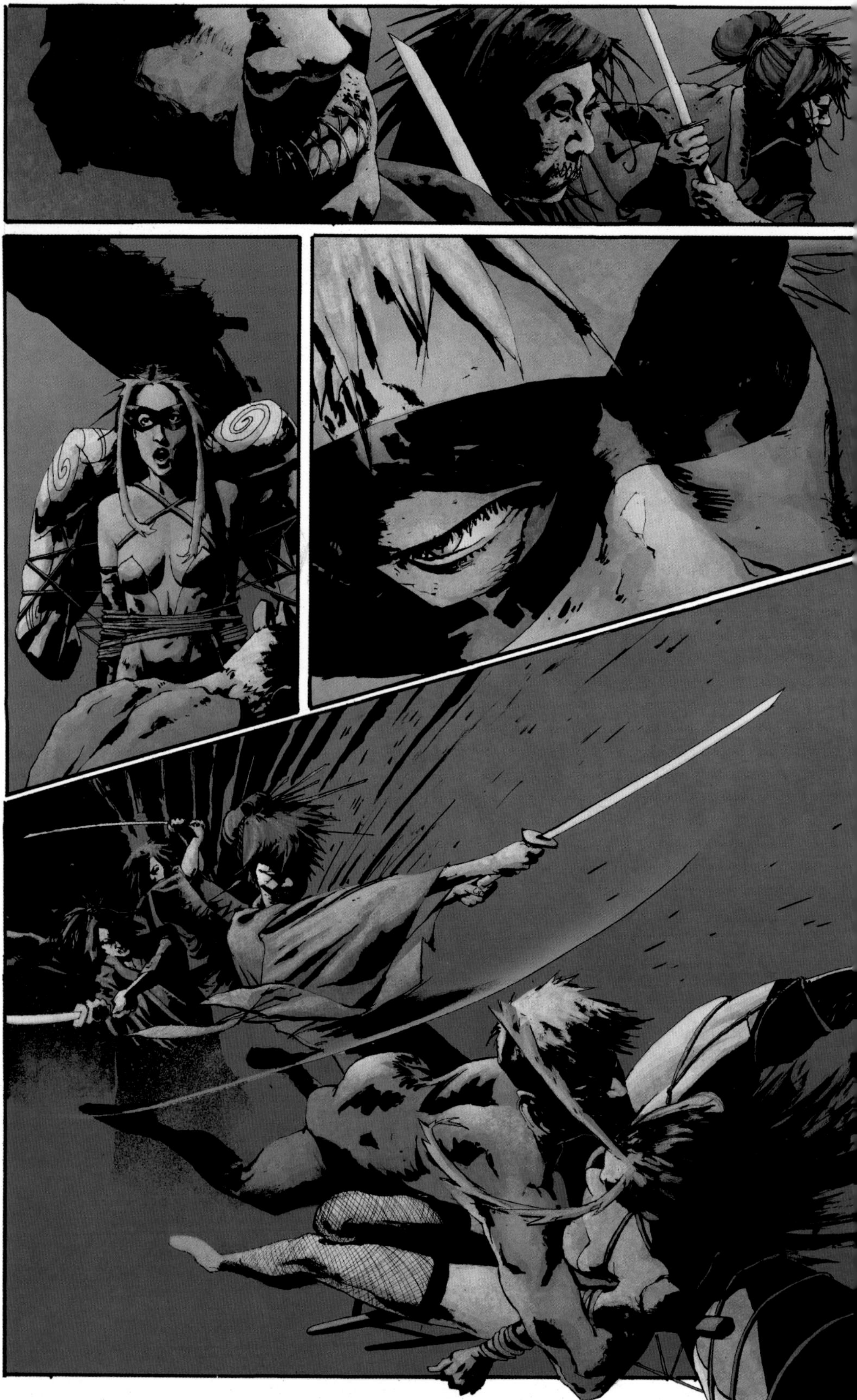

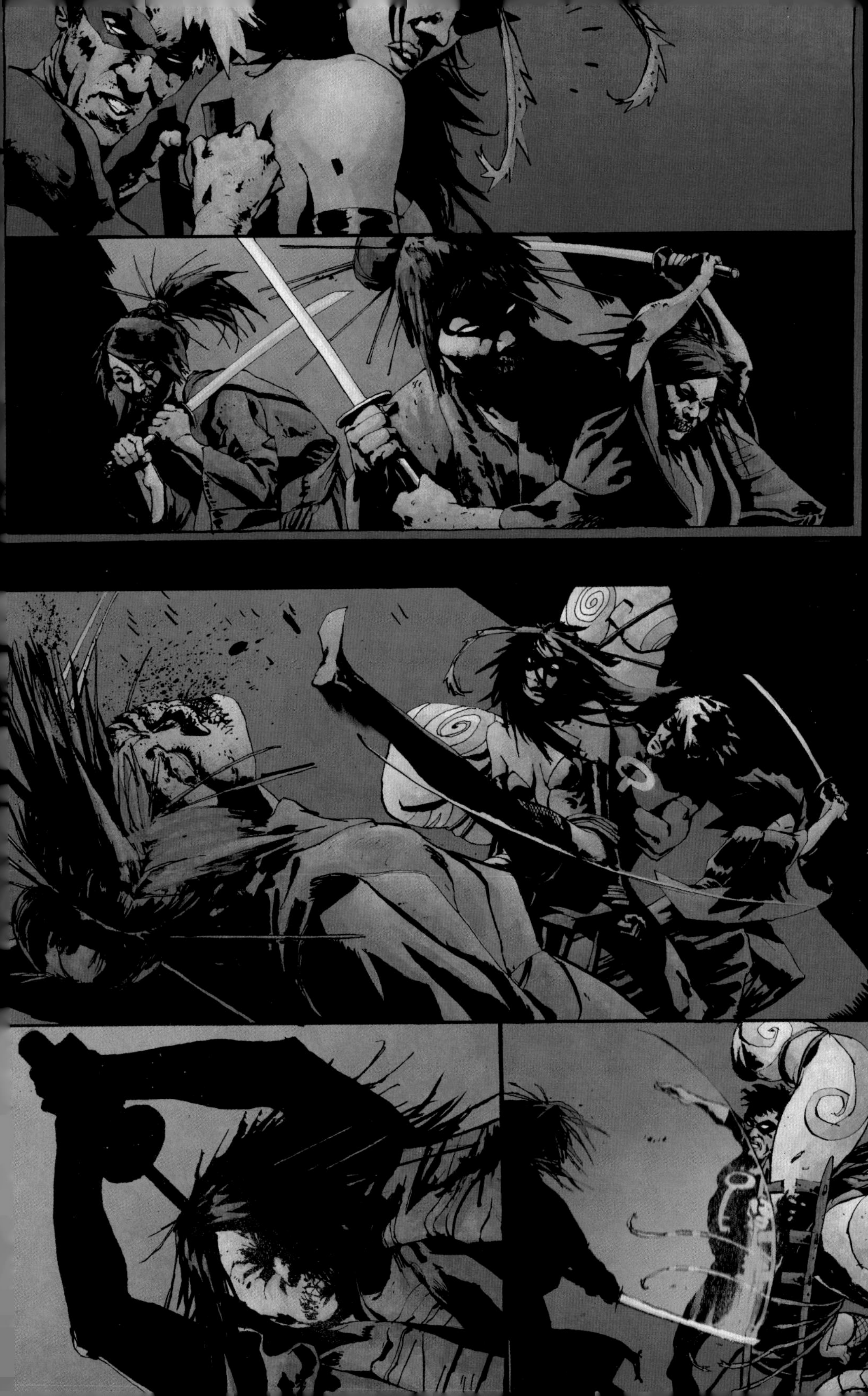

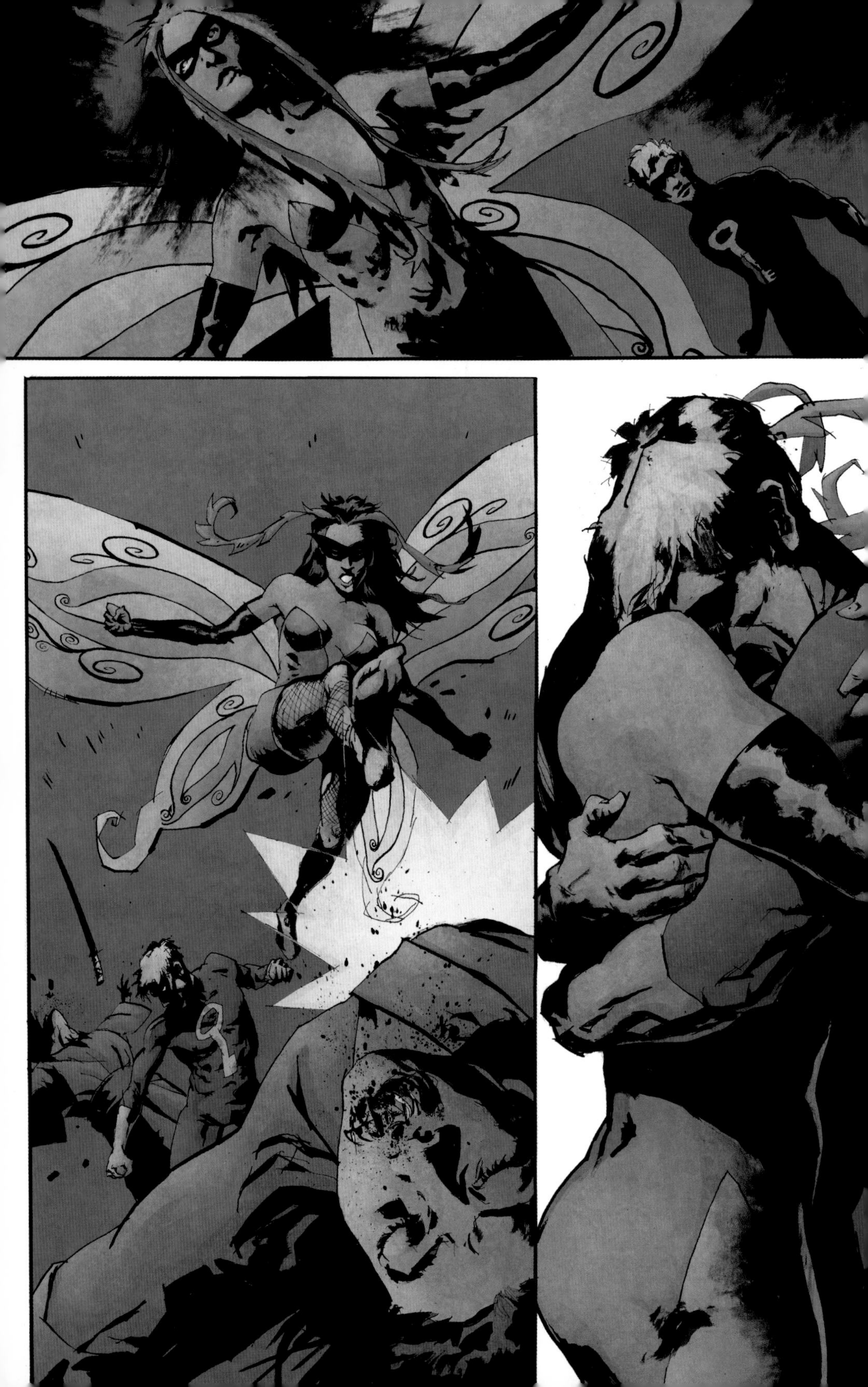

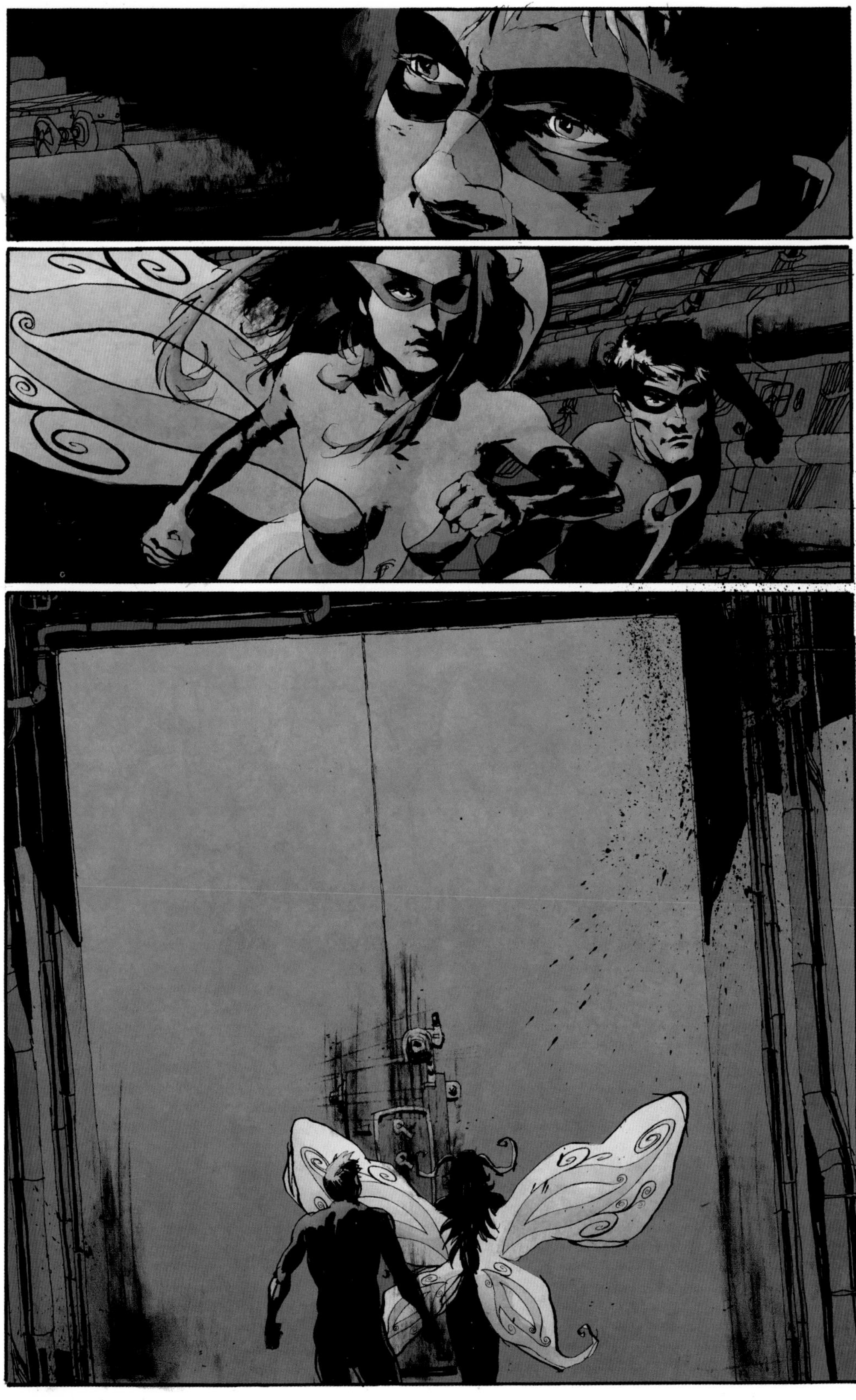

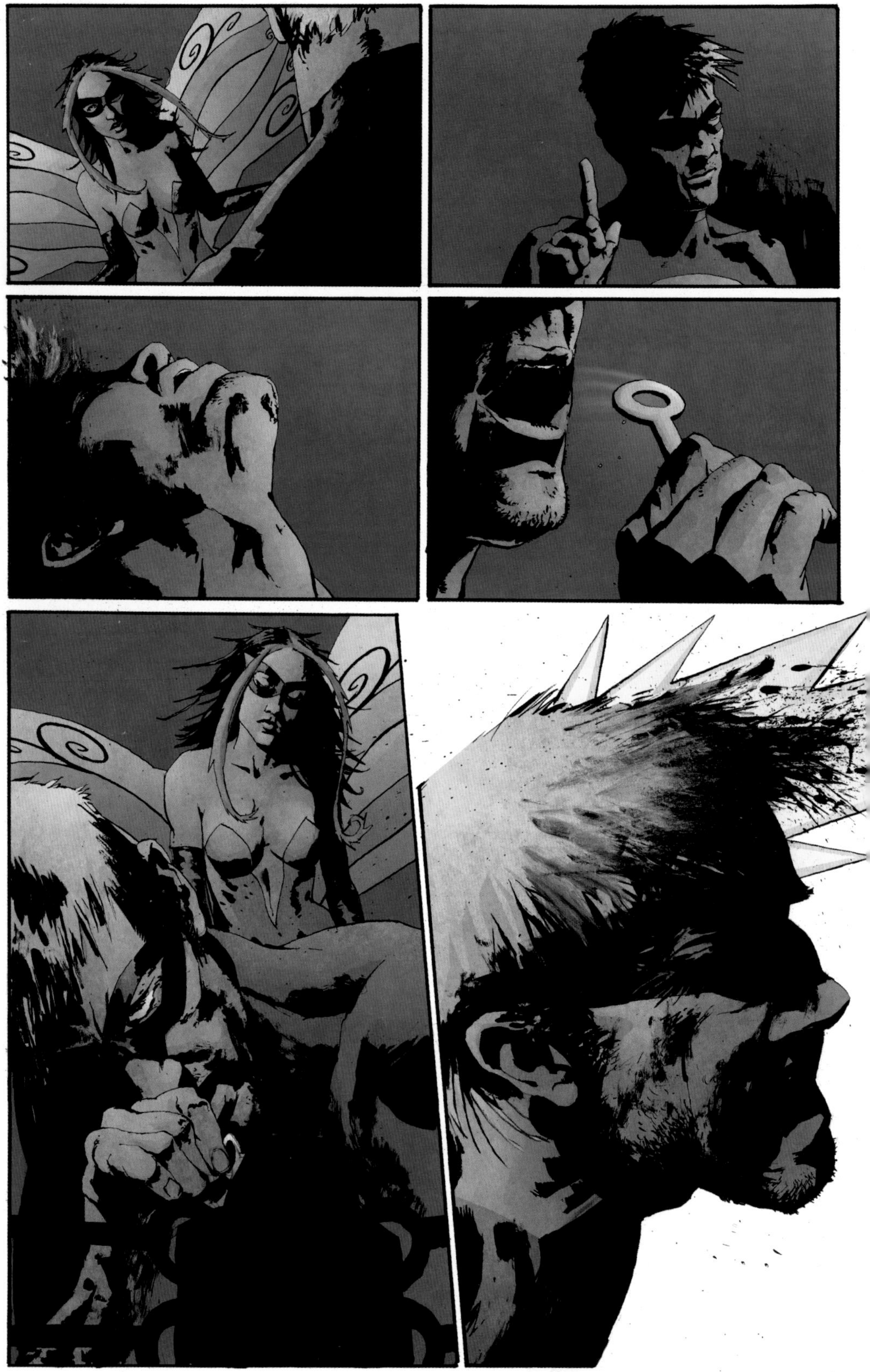

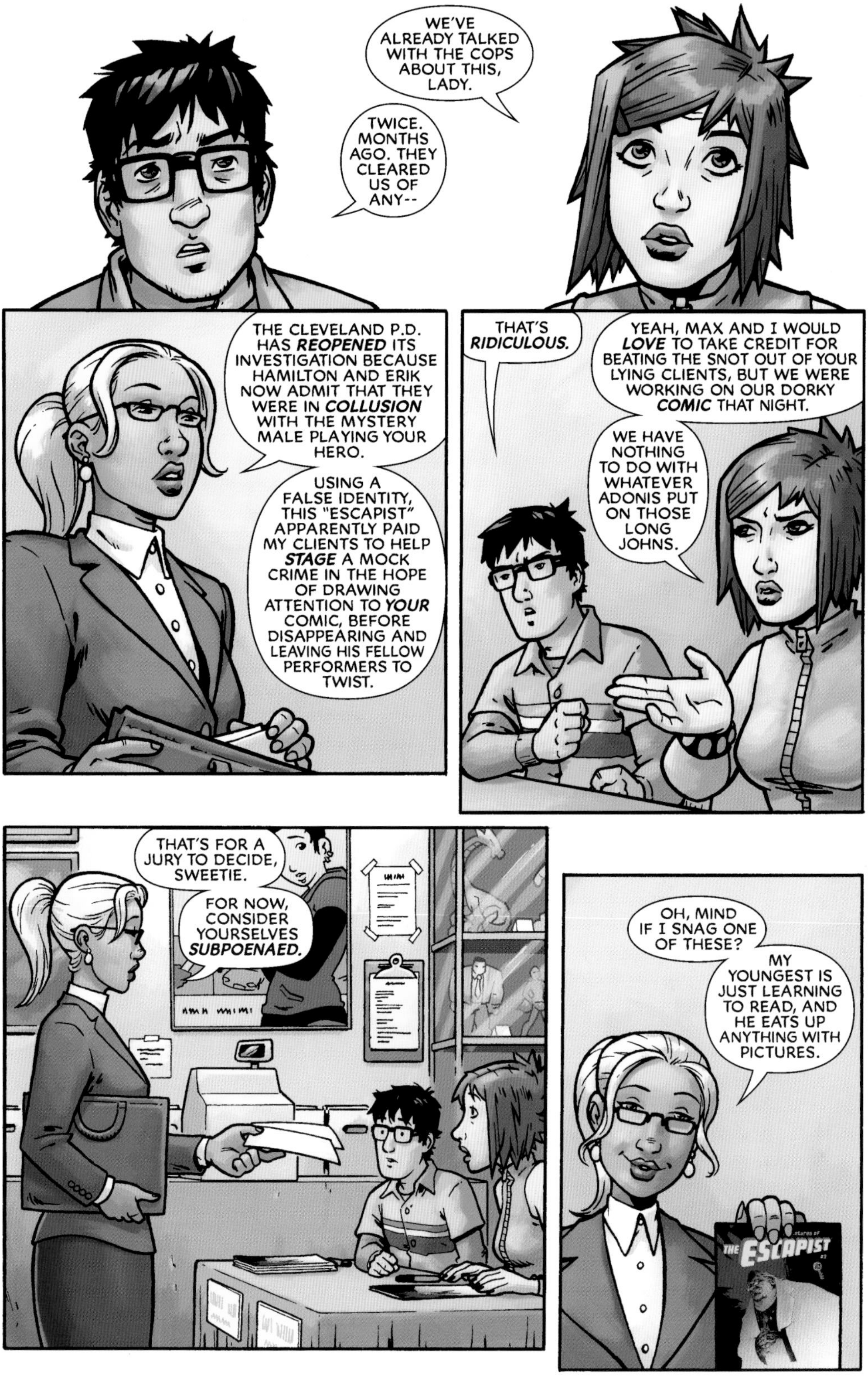
WE'VE ALREADY TALKED WITH THE COPS ABOUT THIS, LADY.
TWICE. MONTHS AGO. THEY CLEARED US OF ANY--
THE CLEVELAND P.D. HAS REOPENED ITS INVESTIGATION BECAUSE HAMILTON AND ERIK NOW ADMIT THAT THEY WERE IN COLLUSION WITH THE MYSTERY MALE PLAYING YOUR HERO.
USING A FALSE IDENTITY, THIS "ESCAPIST" APPARENTLY PAID MY CLIENTS TO HELP STAGE A MOCK CRIME IN THE HOPE OF DRAWING ATTENTION TO YOUR COMIC, BEFORE DISAPPEARING AND LEAVING HIS FELLOW PERFORMERS TO TWIST.
THAT'S RIDICULOUS.
YEAH, MAX AND I WOULD LOVE TO TAKE CREDIT FOR BEATING THE SNOT OUT OF YOUR LYING CLIENTS, BUT WE WERE WORKING ON OUR DORKY COMIC THAT NIGHT.
WE HAVE NOTHING TO DO WITH WHATEVER ADONIS PUT ON THOSE LONG JOHNS.
THAT'S FOR A JURY TO DECIDE, SWEETIE.
FOR NOW, CONSIDER YOURSELVES SUBPOENAED.
OH, MIND IF I SNAG ONE OF THESE?
MY YOUNGEST IS JUST LEARNING TO READ, AND HE EATS UP ANYTHING WITH PICTURES.
THE ESCAPIST

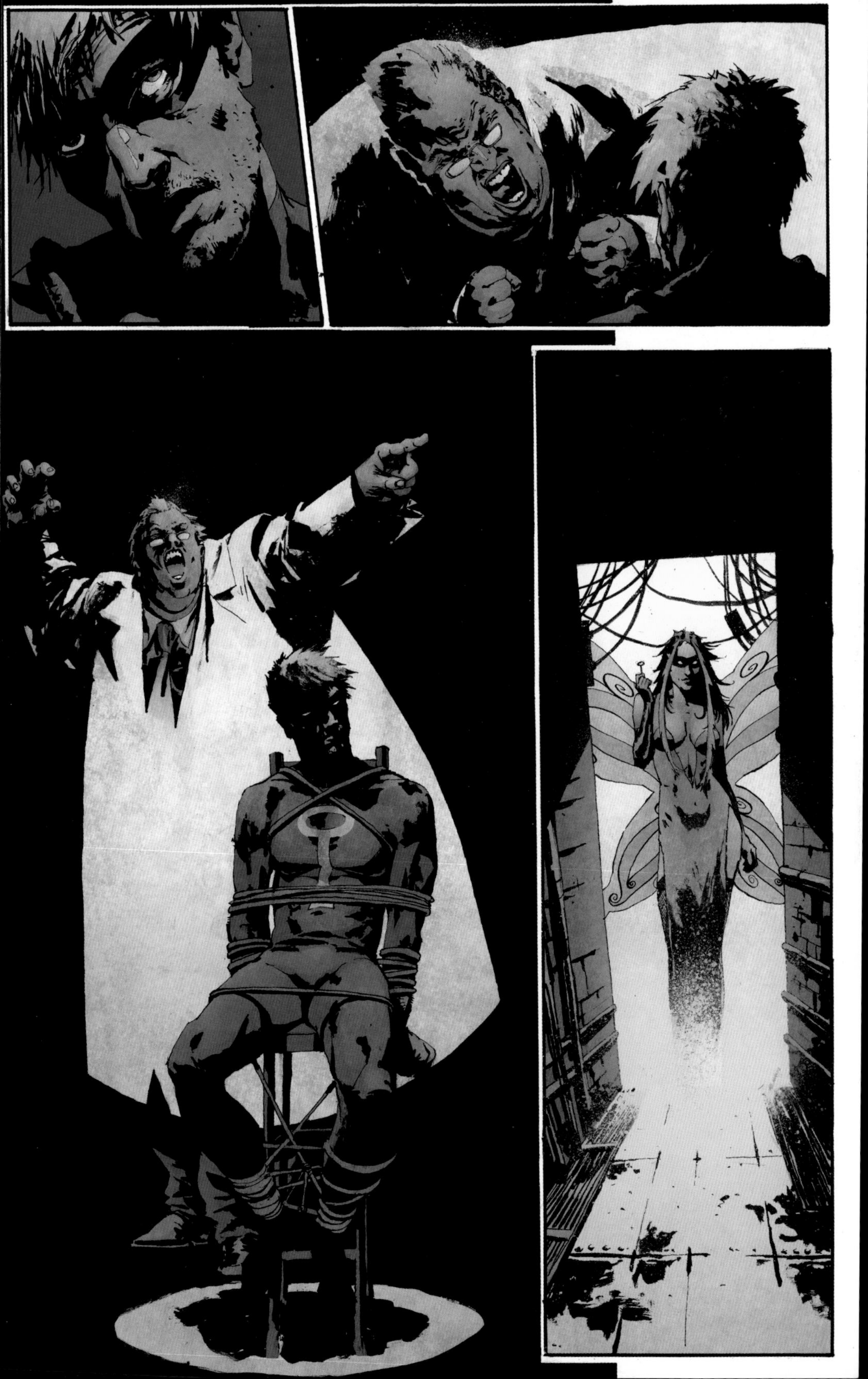

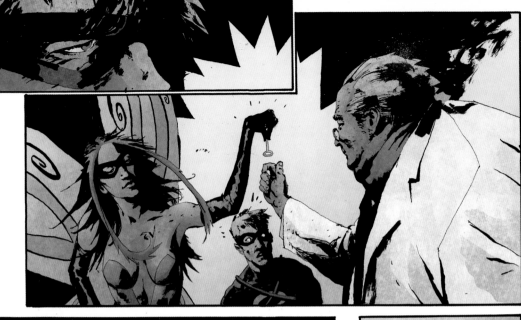

NEXT:
BETRAYED!

109

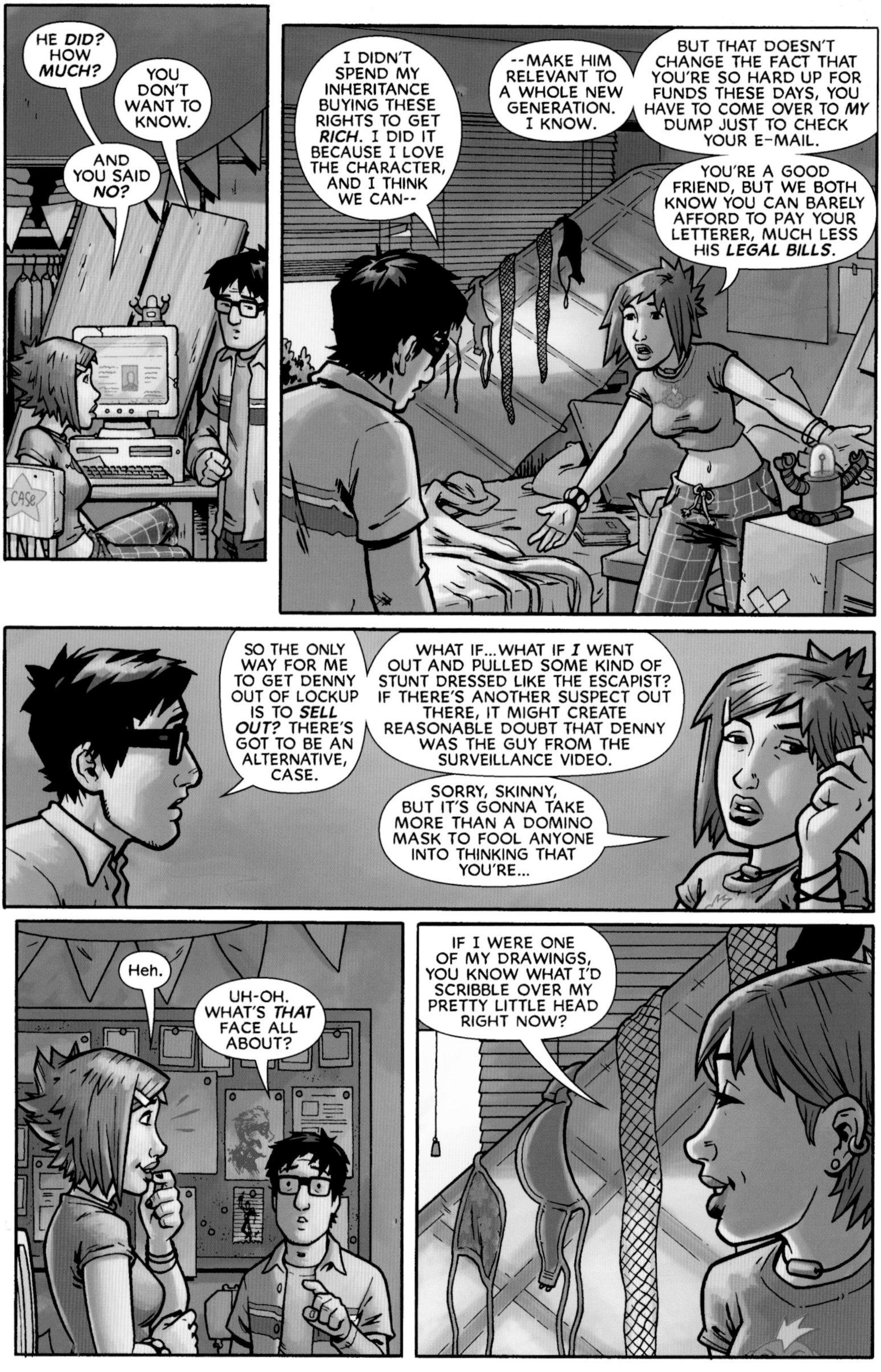
HE DID? HOW MUCH?
YOU DON'T WANT TO KNOW.
AND YOU SAID NO?
I DIDN'T SPEND MY INHERITANCE BUYING THESE RIGHTS TO GET RICH. I DID IT BECAUSE I LOVE THE CHARACTER, AND I THINK WE CAN--
--MAKE HIM RELEVANT TO A WHOLE NEW GENERATION. I KNOW.
BUT THAT DOESN'T CHANGE THE FACT THAT YOU'RE SO HARD UP FOR FUNDS THESE DAYS, YOU HAVE TO COME OVER TO MY DUMP JUST TO CHECK YOUR E-MAIL.
YOU'RE A GOOD FRIEND, BUT WE BOTH KNOW YOU CAN BARELY AFFORD TO PAY YOUR LETTERER, MUCH LESS HIS LEGAL BILLS.
SO THE ONLY WAY FOR ME TO GET DENNY OUT OF LOCKUP IS TO SELL OUT? THERE'S GOT TO BE AN ALTERNATIVE, CASE.
WHAT IF...WHAT IF I WENT OUT AND PULLED SOME KIND OF STUNT DRESSED LIKE THE ESCAPIST? IF THERE'S ANOTHER SUSPECT OUT THERE, IT MIGHT CREATE REASONABLE DOUBT THAT DENNY WAS THE GUY FROM THE SURVEILLANCE VIDEO.
SORRY, SKINNY, BUT IT'S GONNA TAKE MORE THAN A DOMINO MASK TO FOOL ANYONE INTO THINKING THAT YOU'RE...
Heh.
UH-OH. WHAT'S THAT FACE ALL ABOUT?
IF I WERE ONE OF MY DRAWINGS, YOU KNOW WHAT I'D SCRIBBLE OVER MY PRETTY LITTLE HEAD RIGHT NOW?

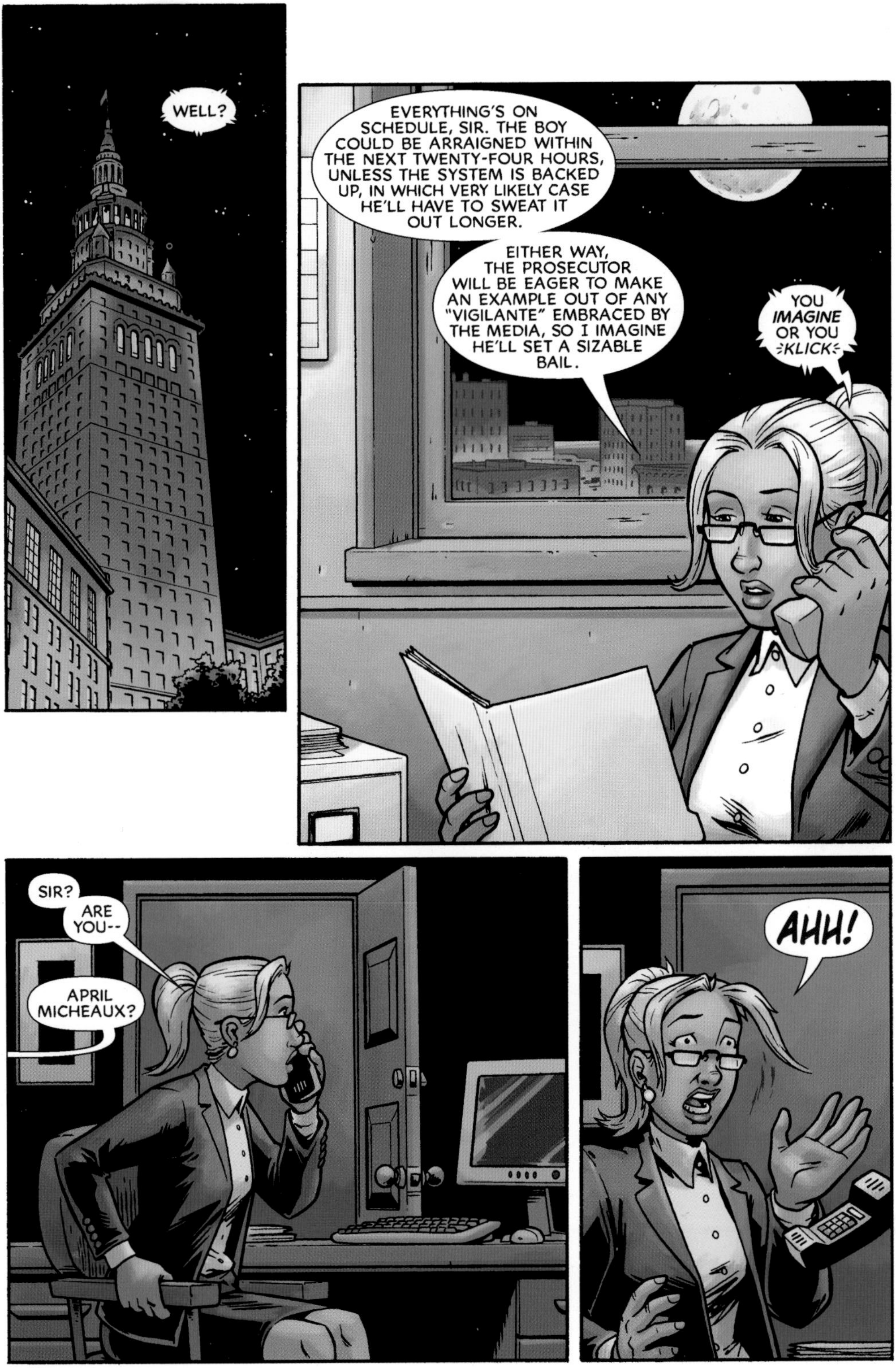
WELL?
EVERYTHING'S ON SCHEDULE, SIR. THE BOY COULD BE ARRAIGNED WITHIN THE NEXT TWENTY-FOUR HOURS, UNLESS THE SYSTEM IS BACKED UP, IN WHICH VERY LIKELY CASE HE'LL HAVE TO SWEAT IT OUT LONGER.
EITHER WAY, THE PROSECUTOR WILL BE EAGER TO MAKE AN EXAMPLE OUT OF ANY "VIGILANTE" EMBRACED BY THE MEDIA, SO I IMAGINE HE'LL SET A SIZABLE BAIL.
YOU *IMAGINE* OR YOU *KLICK*
SIR?
ARE YOU--
APRIL MICHEAUX?
AHH!

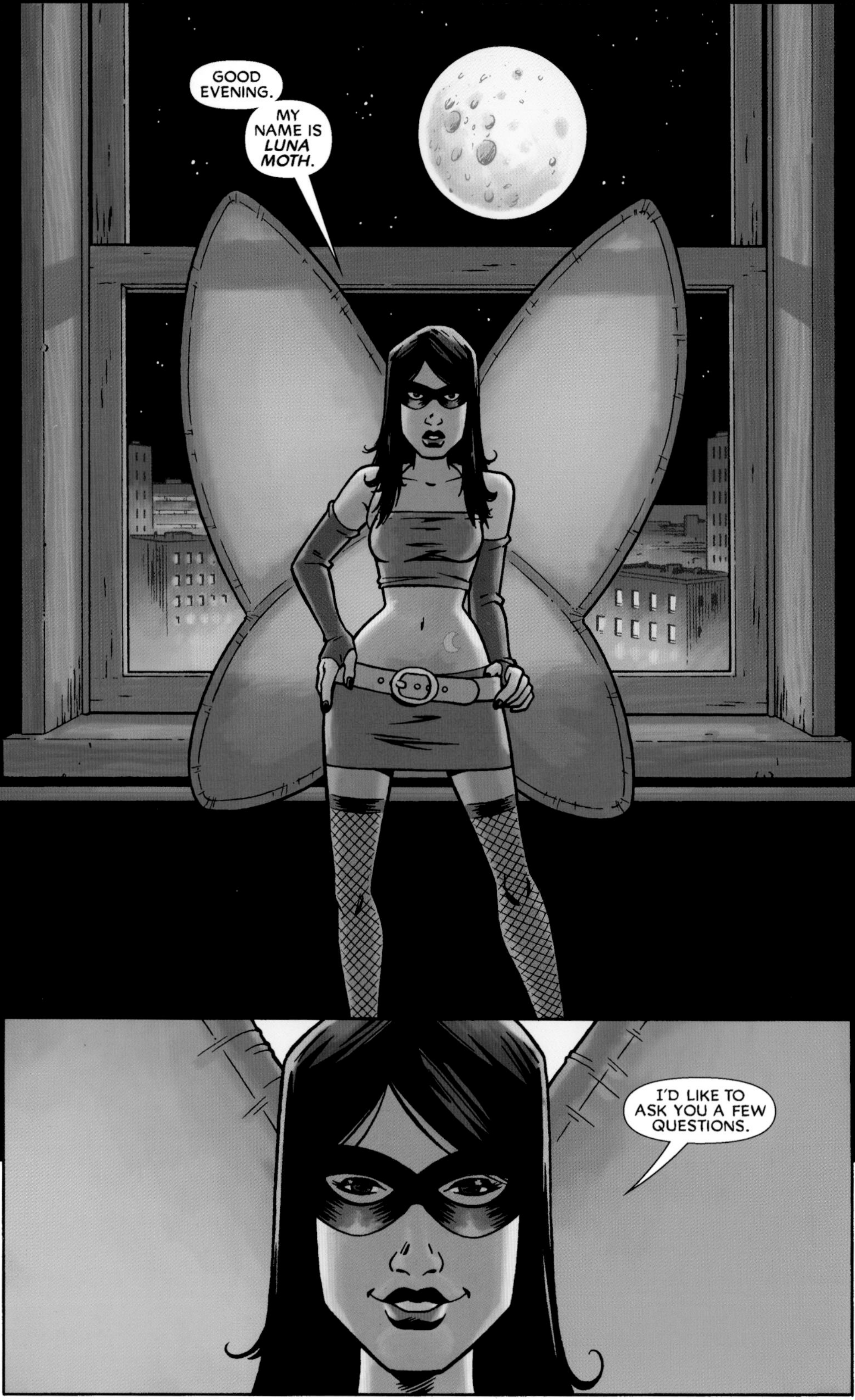
GOOD EVENING.
MY NAME IS *LUNA MOTH*.
I'D LIKE TO ASK YOU A FEW QUESTIONS.

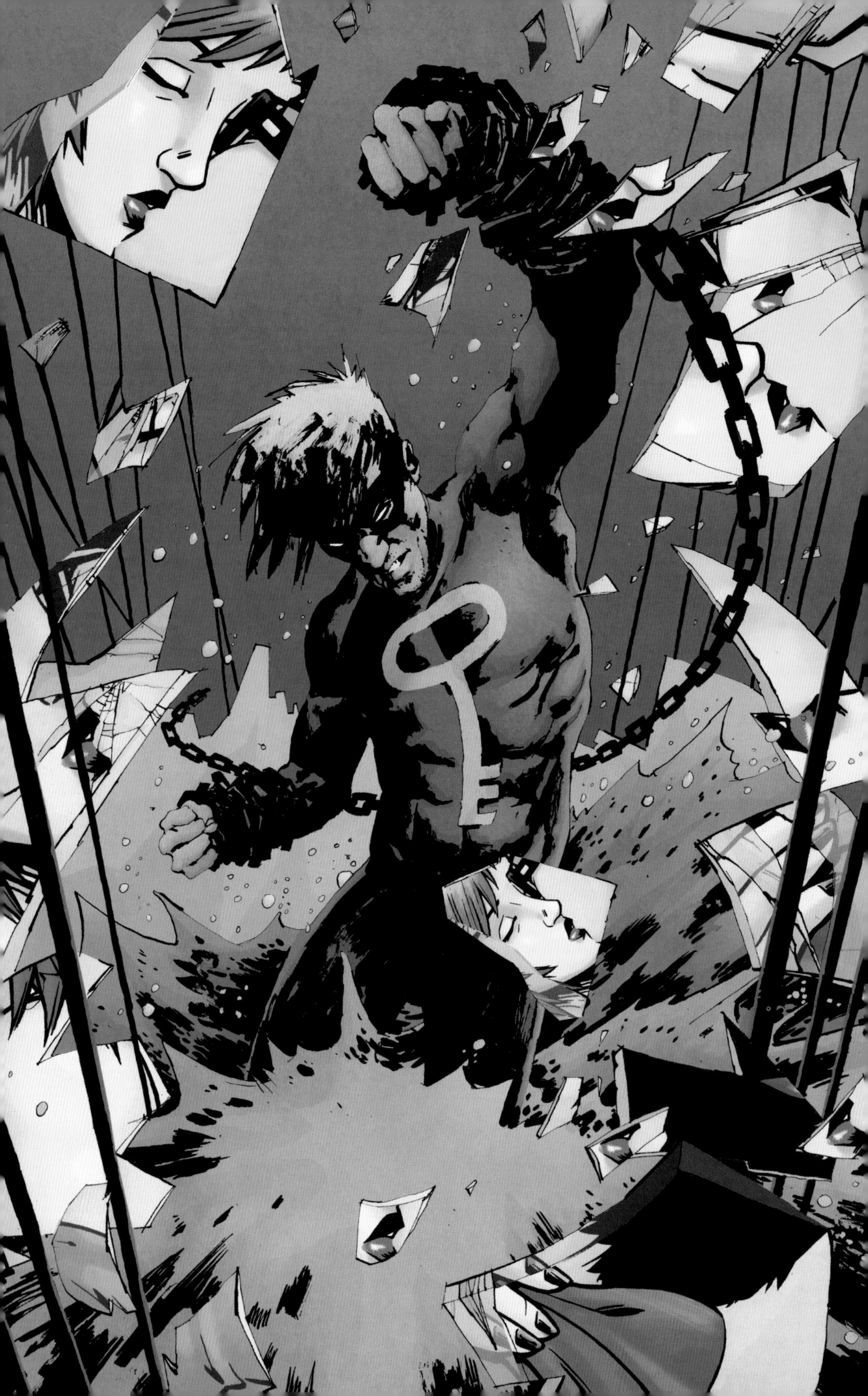

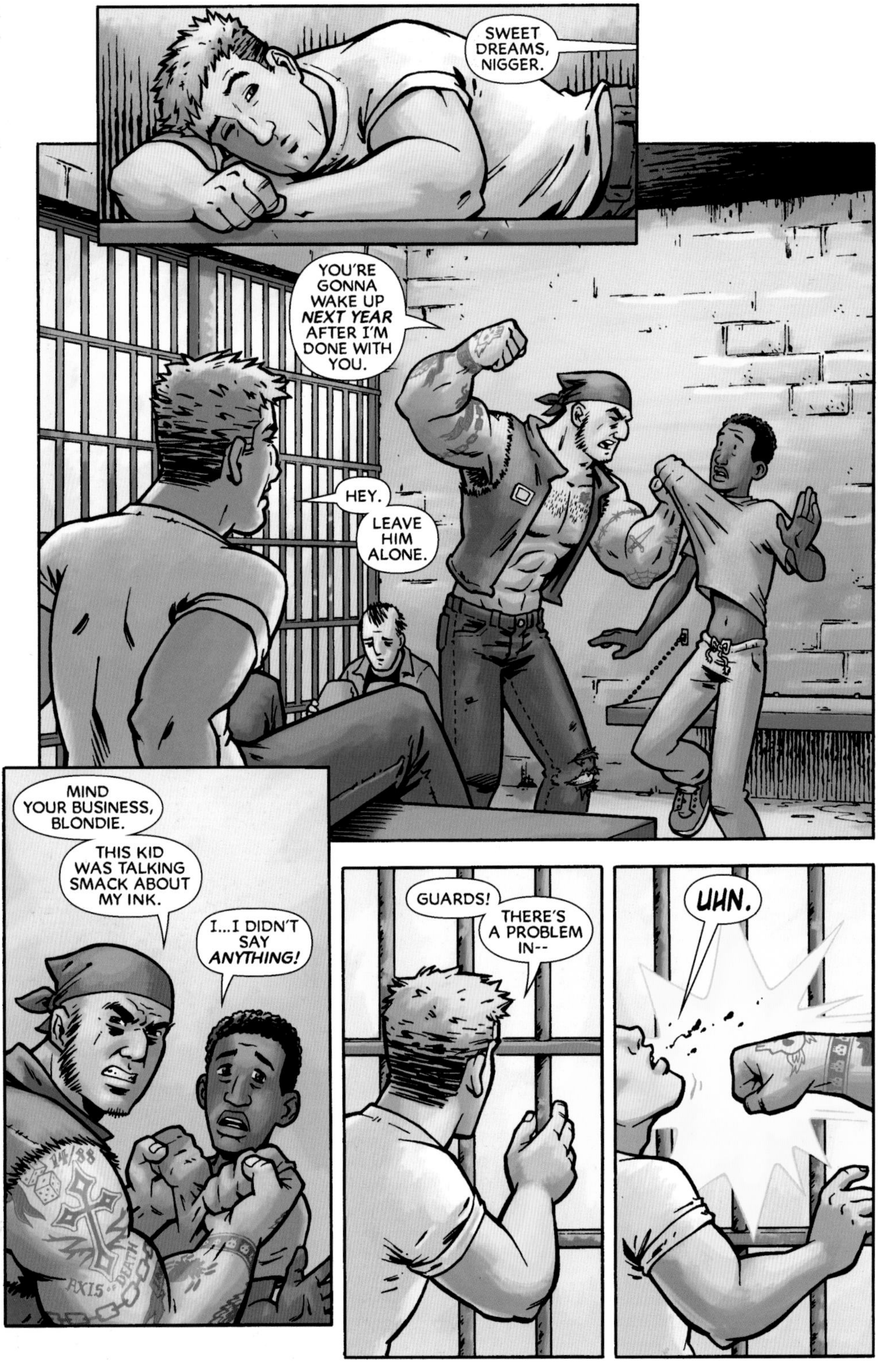
SWEET DREAMS, NIGGER.
YOU'RE GONNA WAKE UP *NEXT YEAR* AFTER I'M DONE WITH YOU.
HEY.
LEAVE HIM ALONE.
MIND YOUR BUSINESS, BLONDIE.
THIS KID WAS TALKING SMACK ABOUT MY INK.
I...I DIDN'T SAY *ANYTHING!*
14/88
AXIS of DEATH
GUARDS!
THERE'S A PROBLEM IN--
UHN.

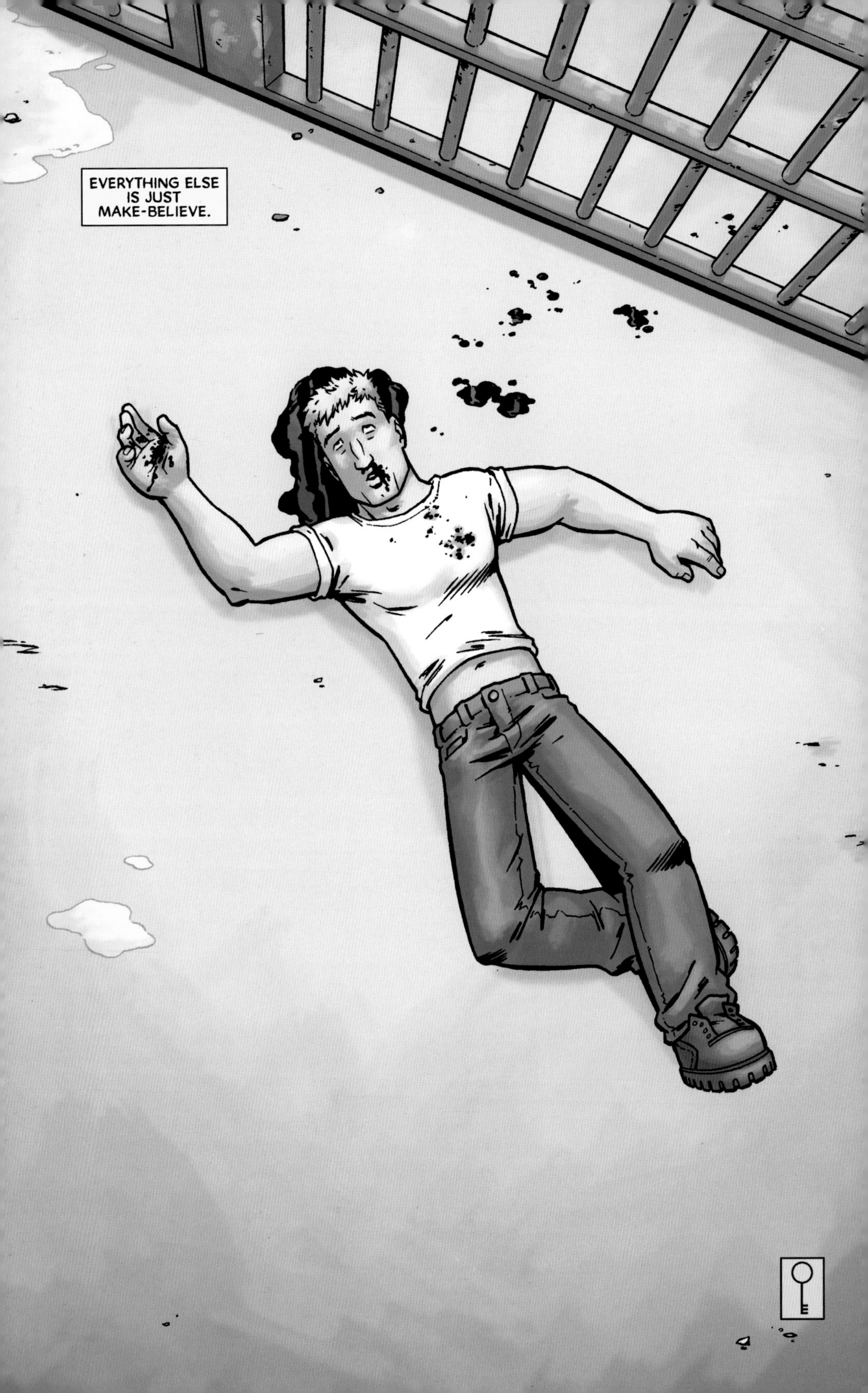
EVERYTHING ELSE IS JUST MAKE-BELIEVE.

134

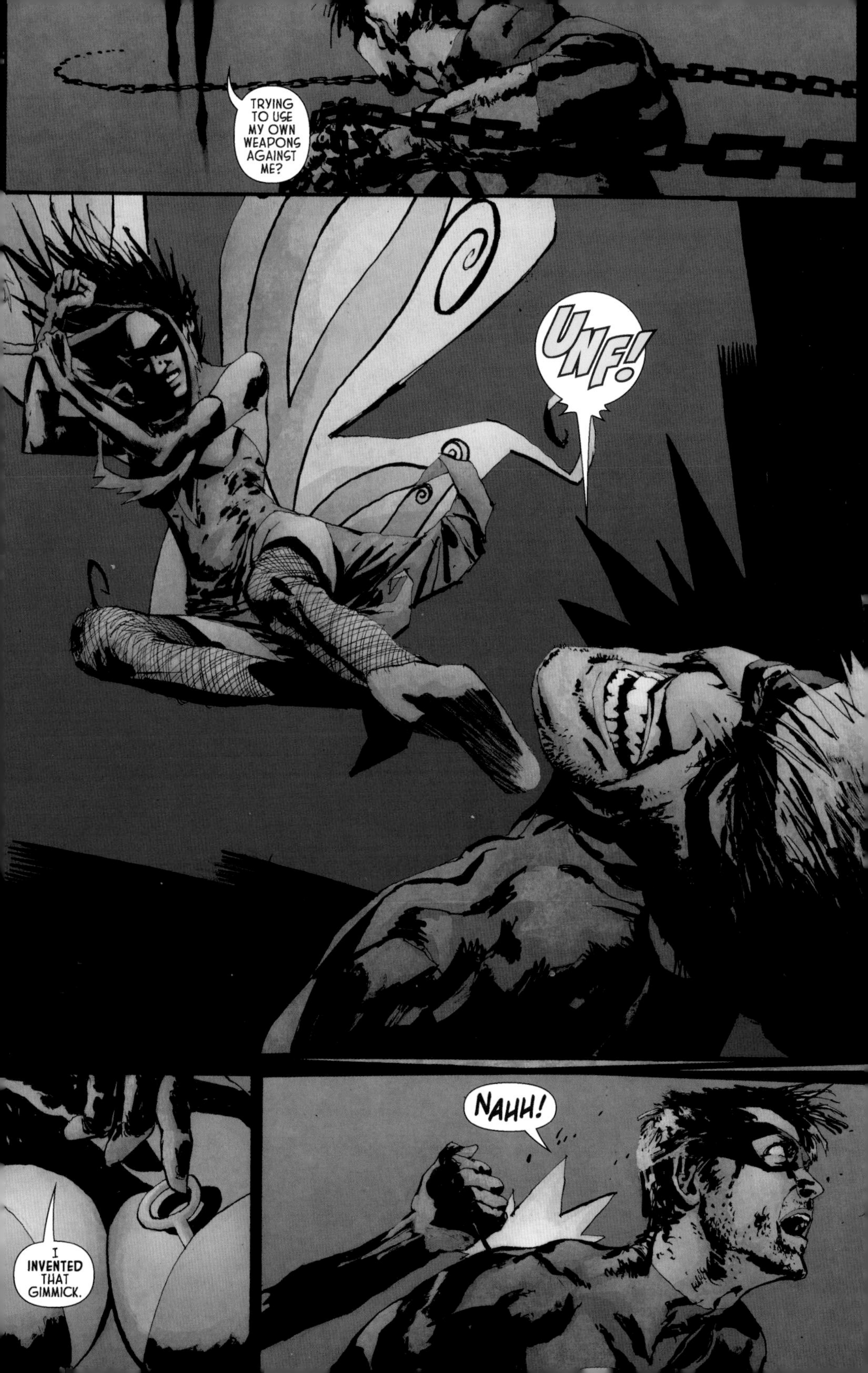
TRYING TO USE MY OWN WEAPONS AGAINST ME?
UNF!
I INVENTED THAT GIMMICK.
NAHH!

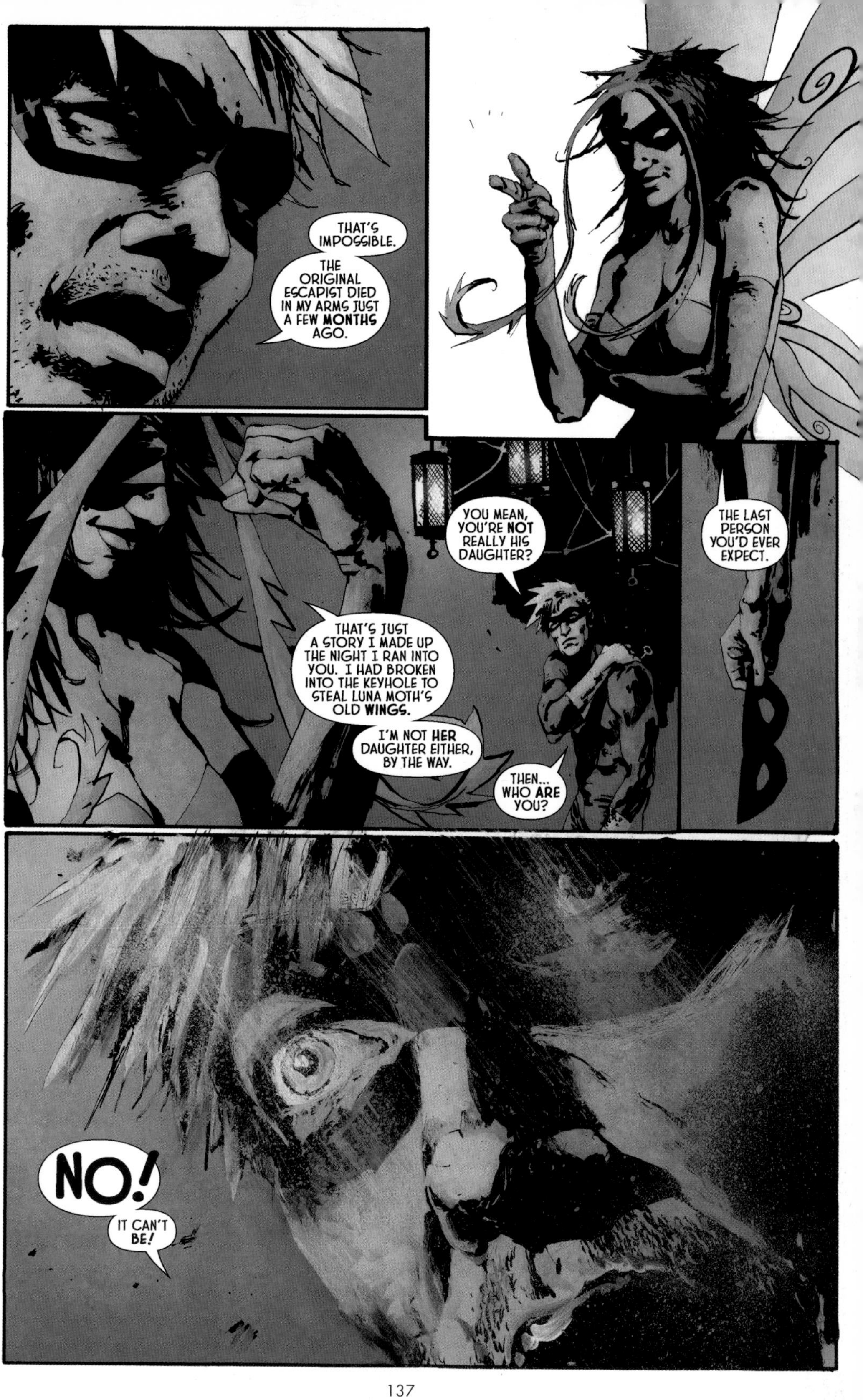
THAT'S IMPOSSIBLE.
THE ORIGINAL ESCAPIST DIED IN MY ARMS JUST A FEW **MONTHS** AGO.
YOU MEAN, YOU'RE **NOT** REALLY HIS DAUGHTER?
THAT'S JUST A STORY I MADE UP THE NIGHT I RAN INTO YOU. I HAD BROKEN INTO THE KEYHOLE TO STEAL LUNA MOTH'S OLD **WINGS**.
I'M NOT **HER** DAUGHTER EITHER, BY THE WAY.
THEN... WHO **ARE** YOU?
THE LAST PERSON YOU'D EVER EXPECT.
NO!
IT CAN'T **BE!**

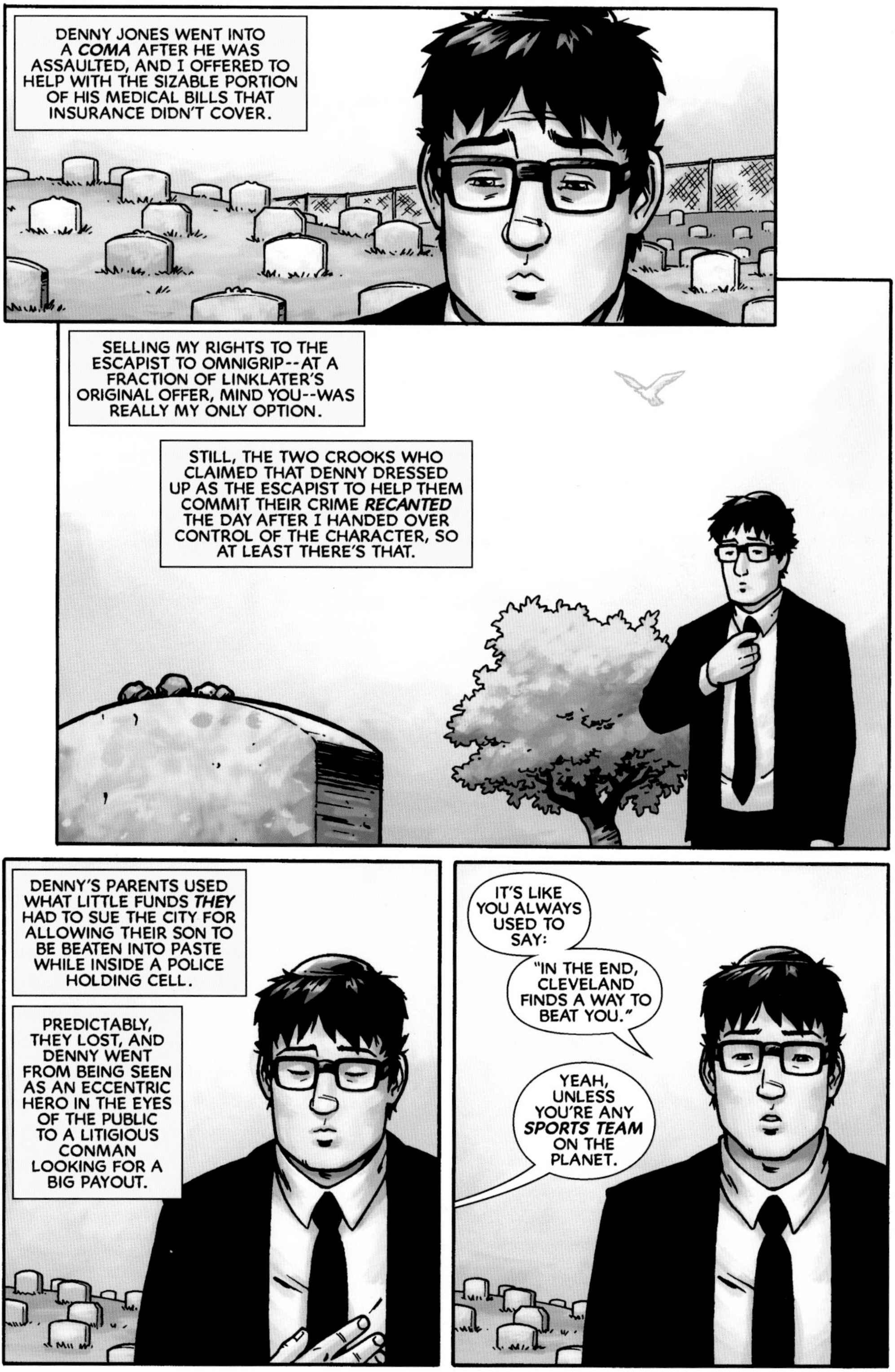
DENNY JONES WENT INTO A *COMA* AFTER HE WAS ASSAULTED, AND I OFFERED TO HELP WITH THE SIZABLE PORTION OF HIS MEDICAL BILLS THAT INSURANCE DIDN'T COVER.
SELLING MY RIGHTS TO THE ESCAPIST TO OMNIGRIP--AT A FRACTION OF LINKLATER'S ORIGINAL OFFER, MIND YOU--WAS REALLY MY ONLY OPTION.
STILL, THE TWO CROOKS WHO CLAIMED THAT DENNY DRESSED UP AS THE ESCAPIST TO HELP THEM COMMIT THEIR CRIME *RECANTED* THE DAY AFTER I HANDED OVER CONTROL OF THE CHARACTER, SO AT LEAST THERE'S THAT.
DENNY'S PARENTS USED WHAT LITTLE FUNDS *THEY* HAD TO SUE THE CITY FOR ALLOWING THEIR SON TO BE BEATEN INTO PASTE WHILE INSIDE A POLICE HOLDING CELL.
PREDICTABLY, THEY LOST, AND DENNY WENT FROM BEING SEEN AS AN ECCENTRIC HERO IN THE EYES OF THE PUBLIC TO A LITIGIOUS CONMAN LOOKING FOR A BIG PAYOUT.
IT'S LIKE YOU ALWAYS USED TO SAY:
"IN THE END, CLEVELAND FINDS A WAY TO BEAT YOU."
YEAH, UNLESS YOU'RE ANY *SPORTS TEAM* ON THE PLANET.

143

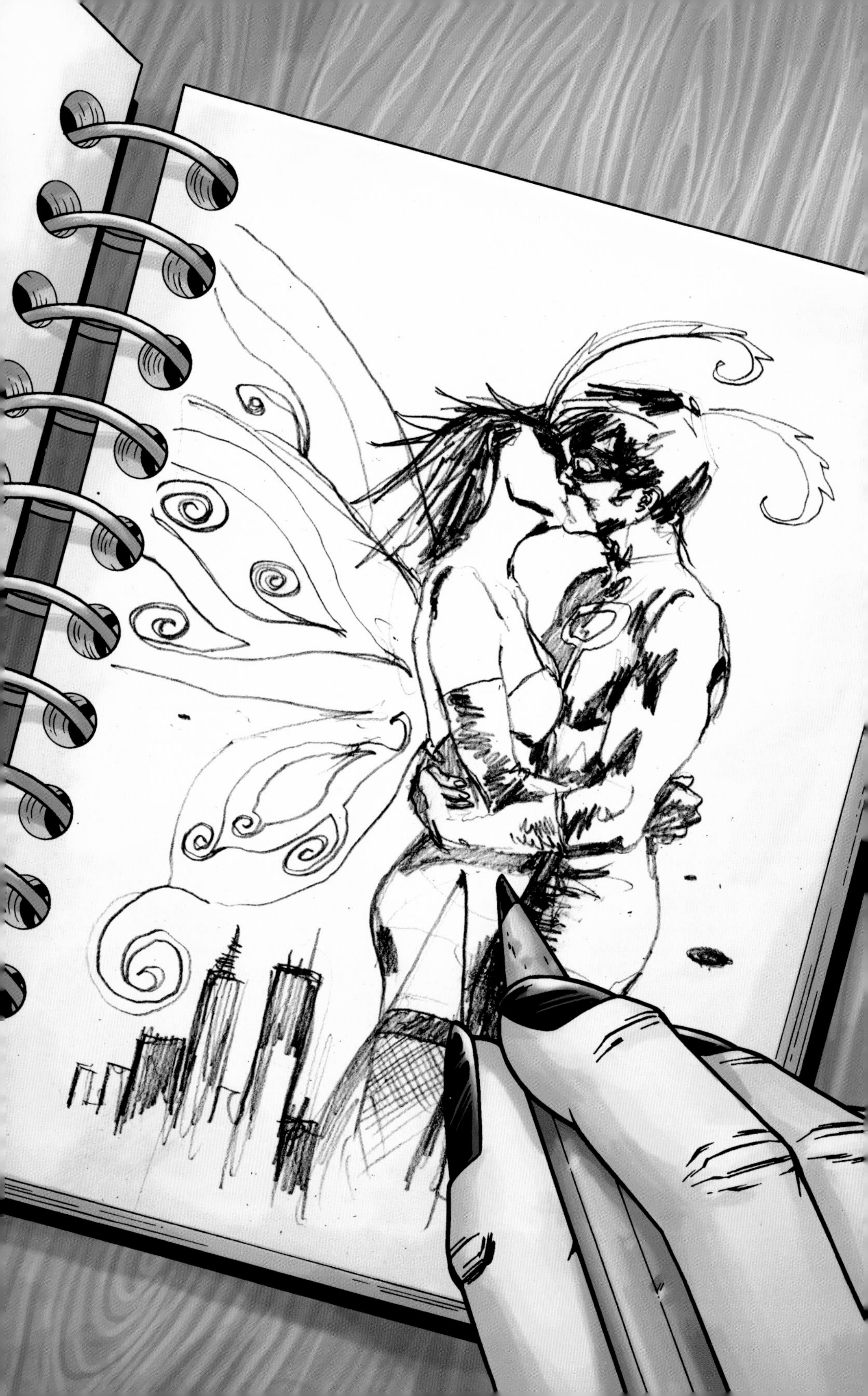

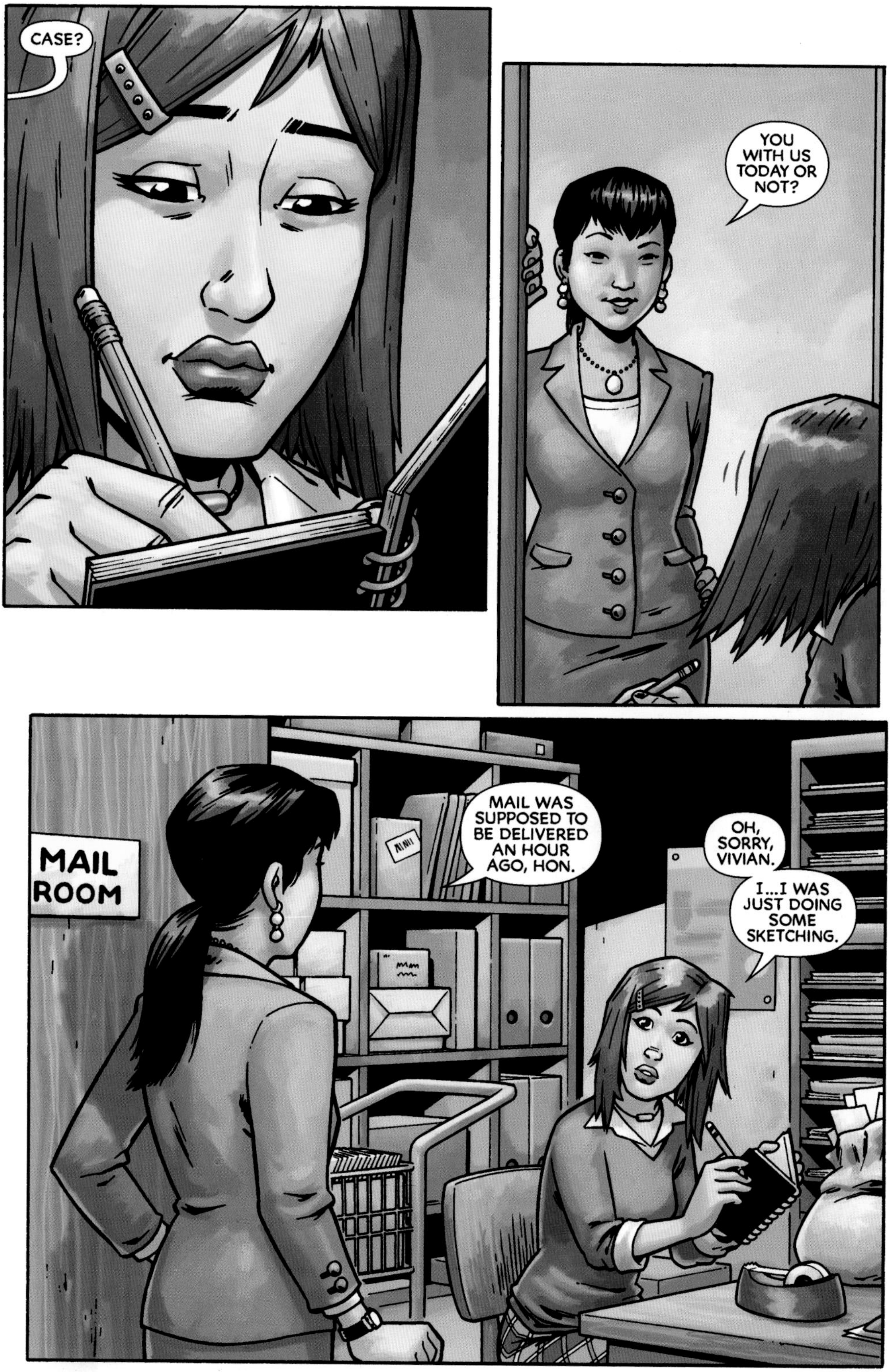
CASE?
YOU WITH US TODAY OR NOT?
MAIL ROOM
MAIL WAS SUPPOSED TO BE DELIVERED AN HOUR AGO, HON.
OH, SORRY, VIVIAN.
I...I WAS JUST DOING SOME SKETCHING.

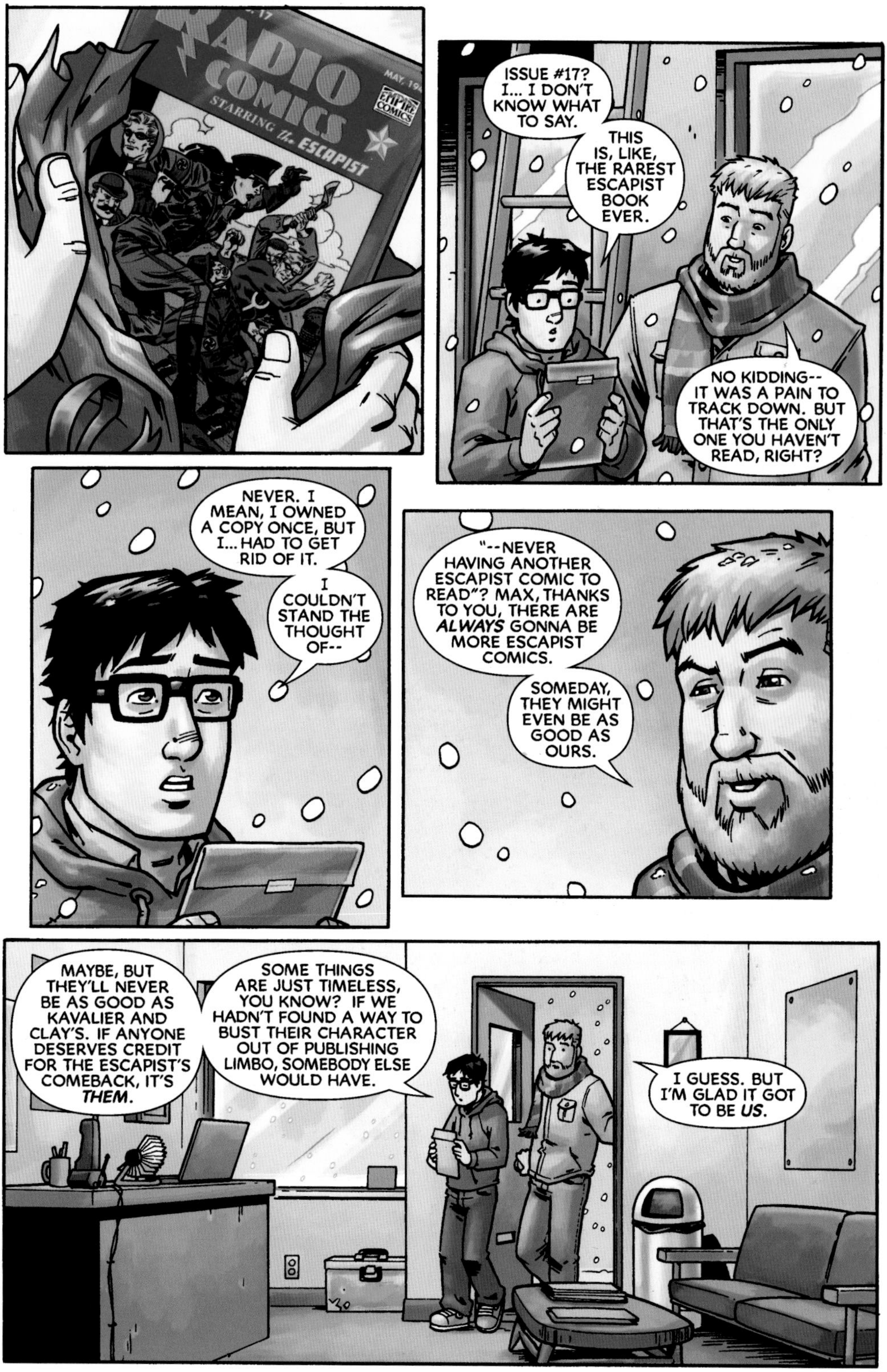
RADIO COMICS
MAY, 194
EMPIRE COMICS
STARRING the ESCAPIST
ISSUE #17? I... I DON'T KNOW WHAT TO SAY.
THIS IS, LIKE, THE RAREST ESCAPIST BOOK EVER.
NO KIDDING-- IT WAS A PAIN TO TRACK DOWN. BUT THAT'S THE ONLY ONE YOU HAVEN'T READ, RIGHT?
NEVER. I MEAN, I OWNED A COPY ONCE, BUT I...HAD TO GET RID OF IT.
I COULDN'T STAND THE THOUGHT OF--
"--NEVER HAVING ANOTHER ESCAPIST COMIC TO READ"? MAX, THANKS TO YOU, THERE ARE *ALWAYS* GONNA BE MORE ESCAPIST COMICS.
SOMEDAY, THEY MIGHT EVEN BE AS GOOD AS OURS.
MAYBE, BUT THEY'LL NEVER BE AS GOOD AS KAVALIER AND CLAY'S. IF ANYONE DESERVES CREDIT FOR THE ESCAPIST'S COMEBACK, IT'S *THEM*.
SOME THINGS ARE JUST TIMELESS, YOU KNOW? IF WE HADN'T FOUND A WAY TO BUST THEIR CHARACTER OUT OF PUBLISHING LIMBO, SOMEBODY ELSE WOULD HAVE.
I GUESS. BUT I'M GLAD IT GOT TO BE *US*.

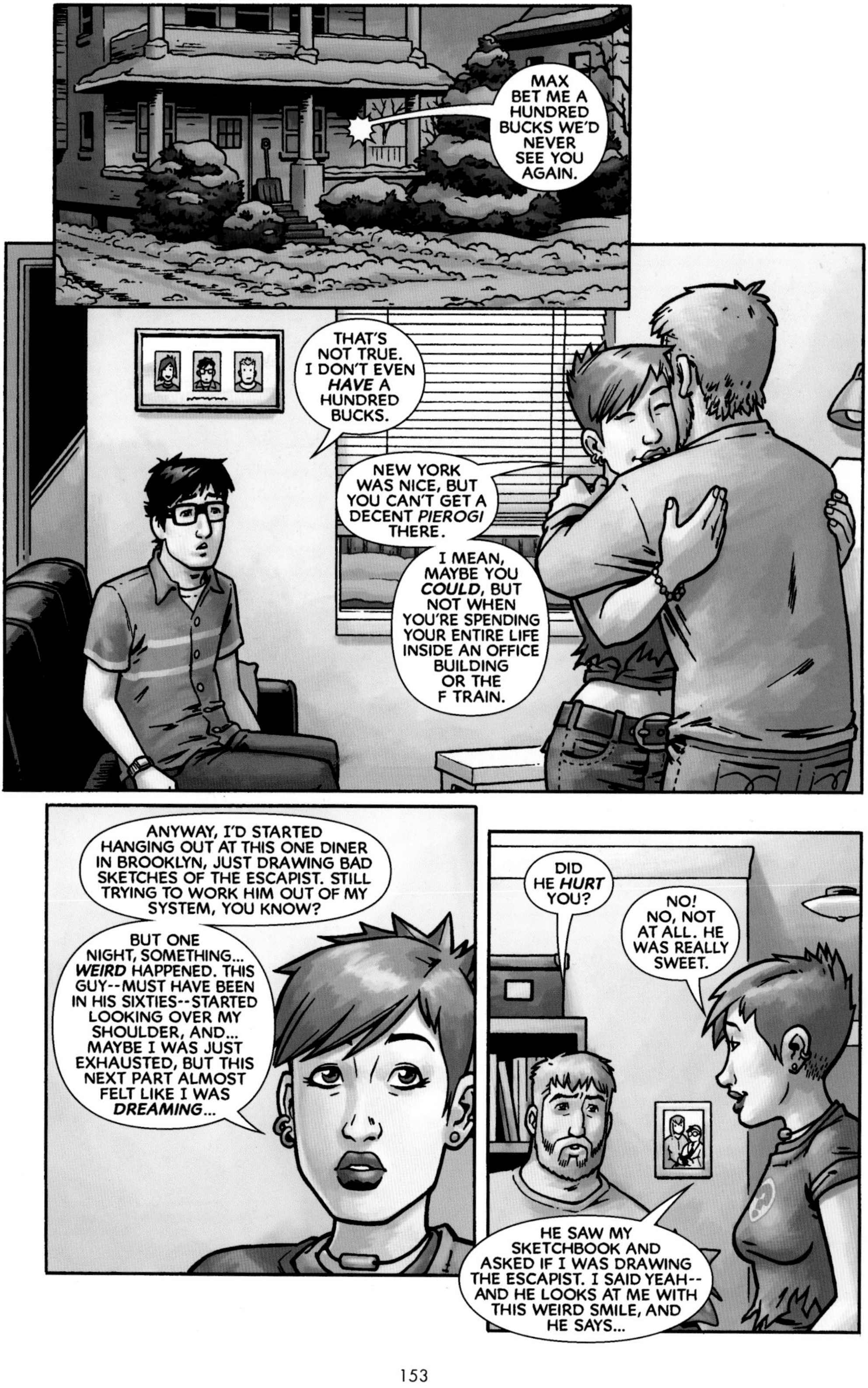
MAX BET ME A HUNDRED BUCKS WE'D NEVER SEE YOU AGAIN.
THAT'S NOT TRUE. I DON'T EVEN *HAVE* A HUNDRED BUCKS.
NEW YORK WAS NICE, BUT YOU CAN'T GET A DECENT *PIEROGI* THERE.
I MEAN, MAYBE YOU *COULD*, BUT NOT WHEN YOU'RE SPENDING YOUR ENTIRE LIFE INSIDE AN OFFICE BUILDING OR THE F TRAIN.
ANYWAY, I'D STARTED HANGING OUT AT THIS ONE DINER IN BROOKLYN, JUST DRAWING BAD SKETCHES OF THE ESCAPIST. STILL TRYING TO WORK HIM OUT OF MY SYSTEM, YOU KNOW?
BUT ONE NIGHT, SOMETHING... *WEIRD* HAPPENED. THIS GUY--MUST HAVE BEEN IN HIS SIXTIES--STARTED LOOKING OVER MY SHOULDER, AND... MAYBE I WAS JUST EXHAUSTED, BUT THIS NEXT PART ALMOST FELT LIKE I WAS *DREAMING*...
DID HE *HURT* YOU?
NO! NO, NOT AT ALL. HE WAS REALLY SWEET.
HE SAW MY SKETCHBOOK AND ASKED IF I WAS DRAWING THE ESCAPIST. I SAID YEAH-- AND HE LOOKS AT ME WITH THIS WEIRD SMILE, AND HE SAYS...

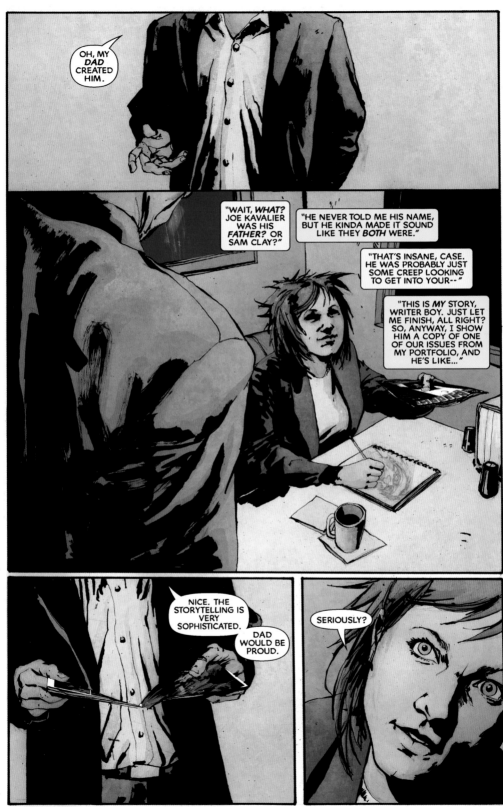

154

...I JUST SEE
FREEDOM.

COVER GALLERY

THE FOLLOWING PAGES feature the front cover artwork from issue eight of *Michael Chabon Presents the Amazing Adventures of The Escapist* and issues one through six of *The Escapists* comic book series.

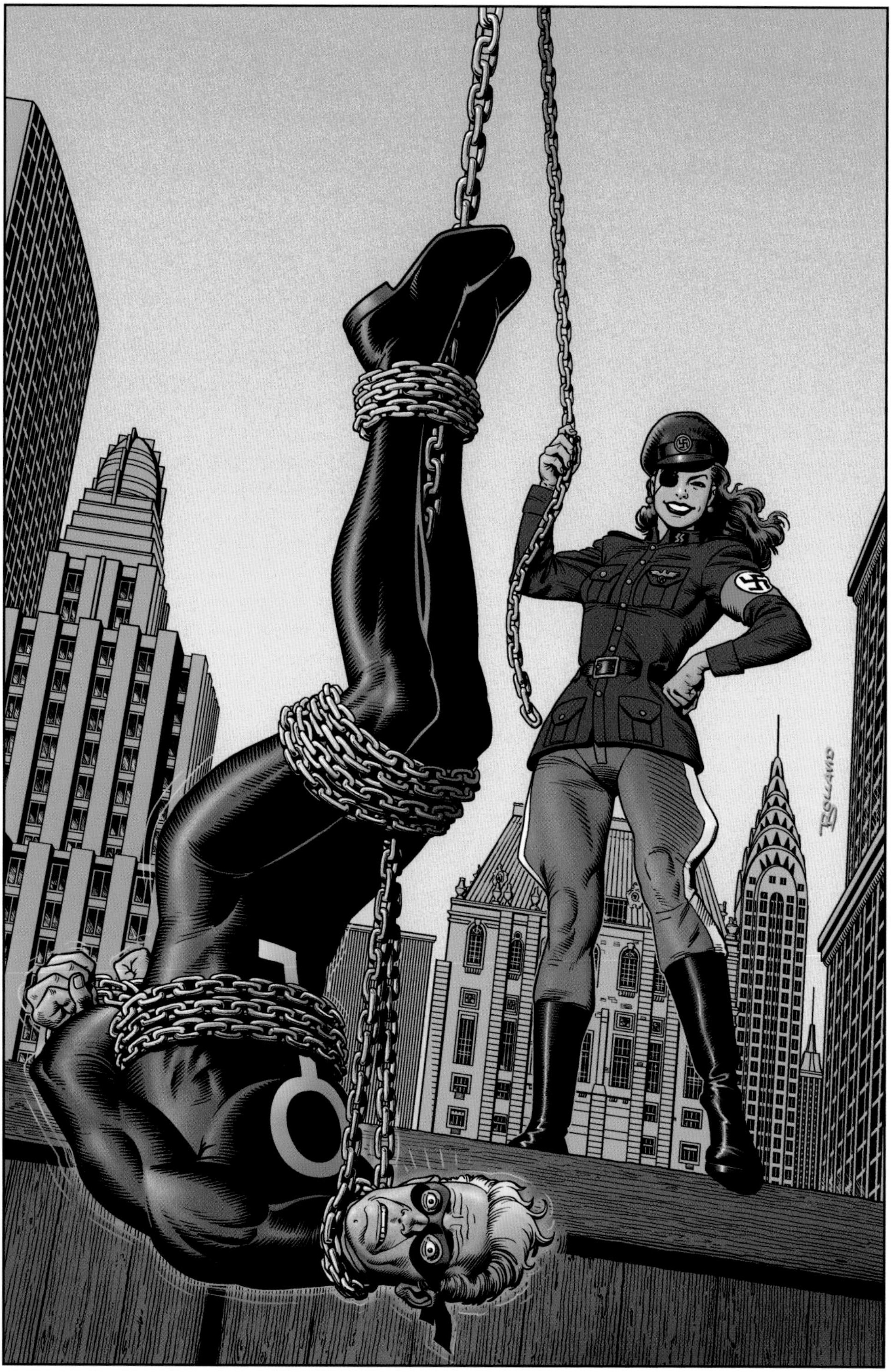
BOLLAND

BRIAN BOLLAND

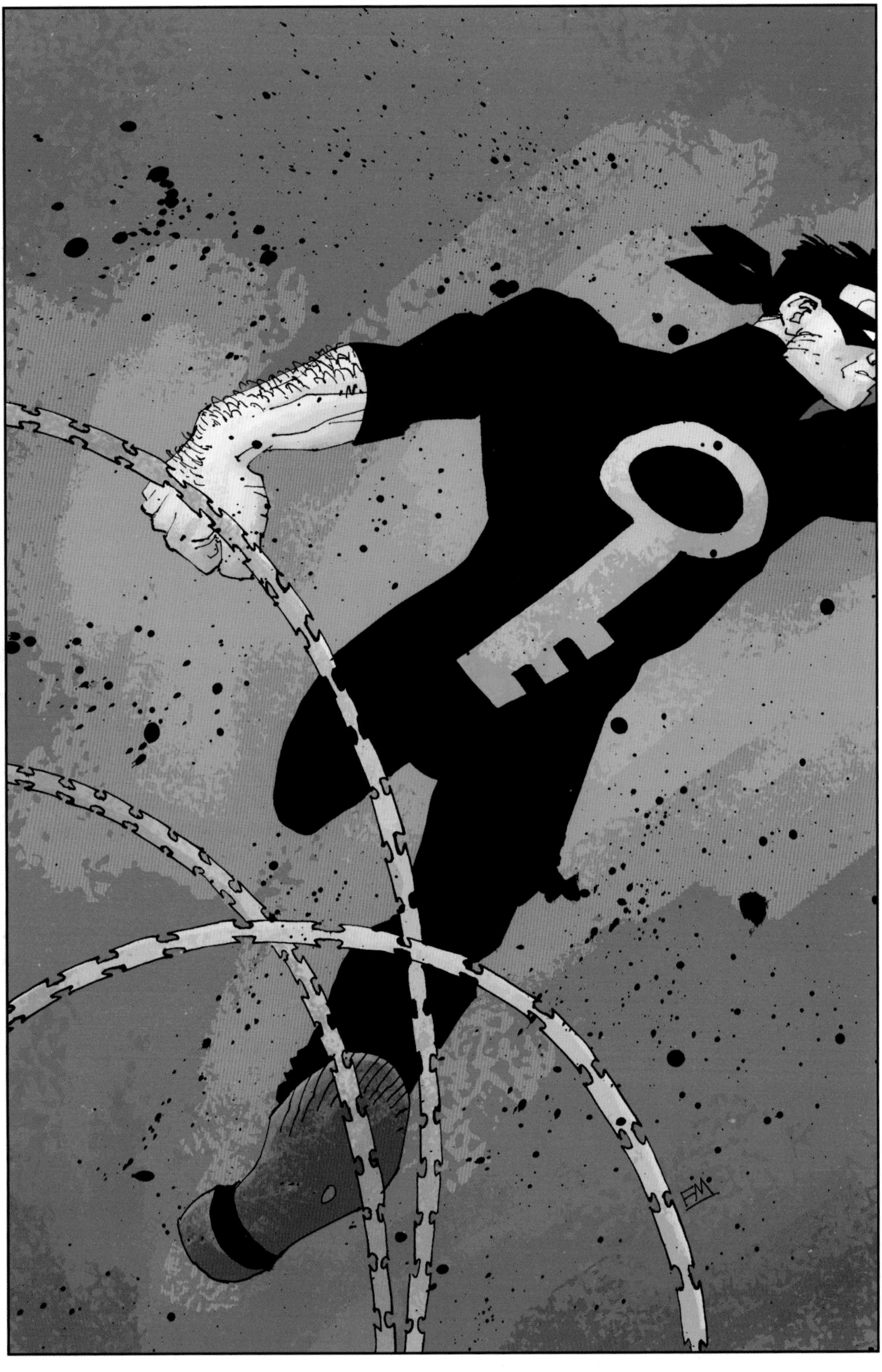

FRANK MILLER • Color by Dave Stewart

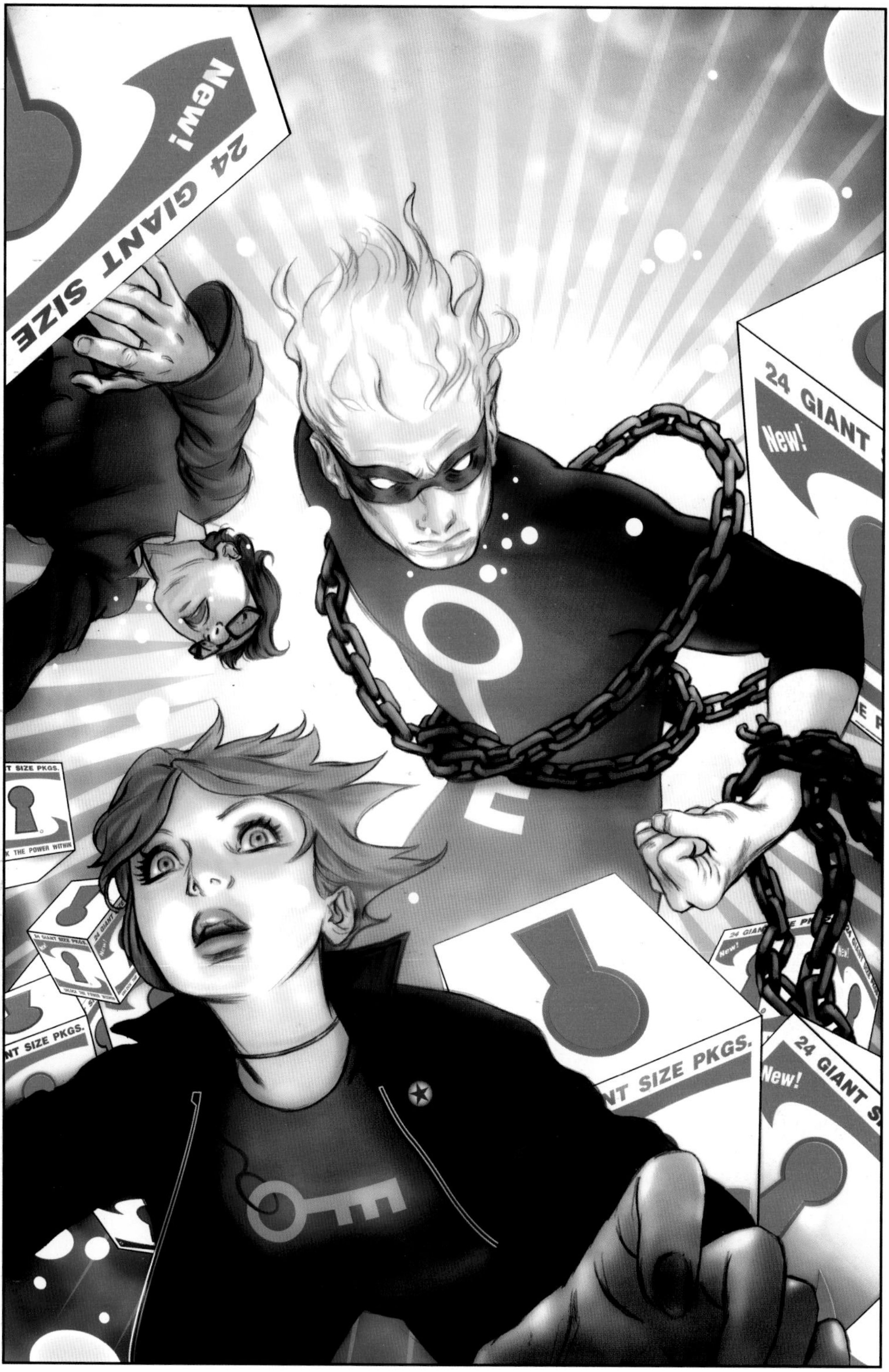

24 GIANT SIZE
New!
24 GIANT
New!
NT SIZE PKGS.
24 GIANT S
New!

JAMES JEAN

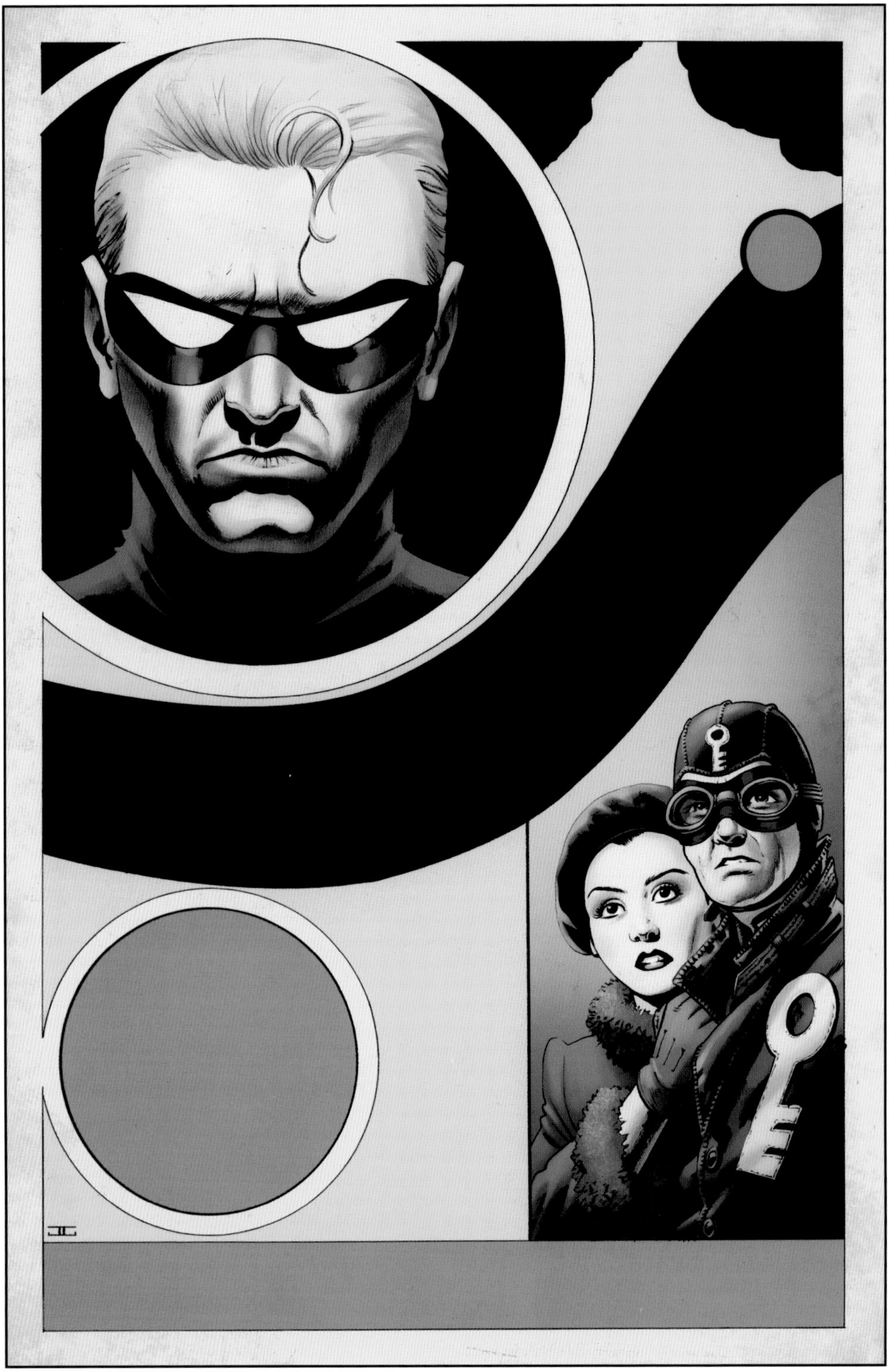

JOHN CASSADAY • Color by Laura Martin

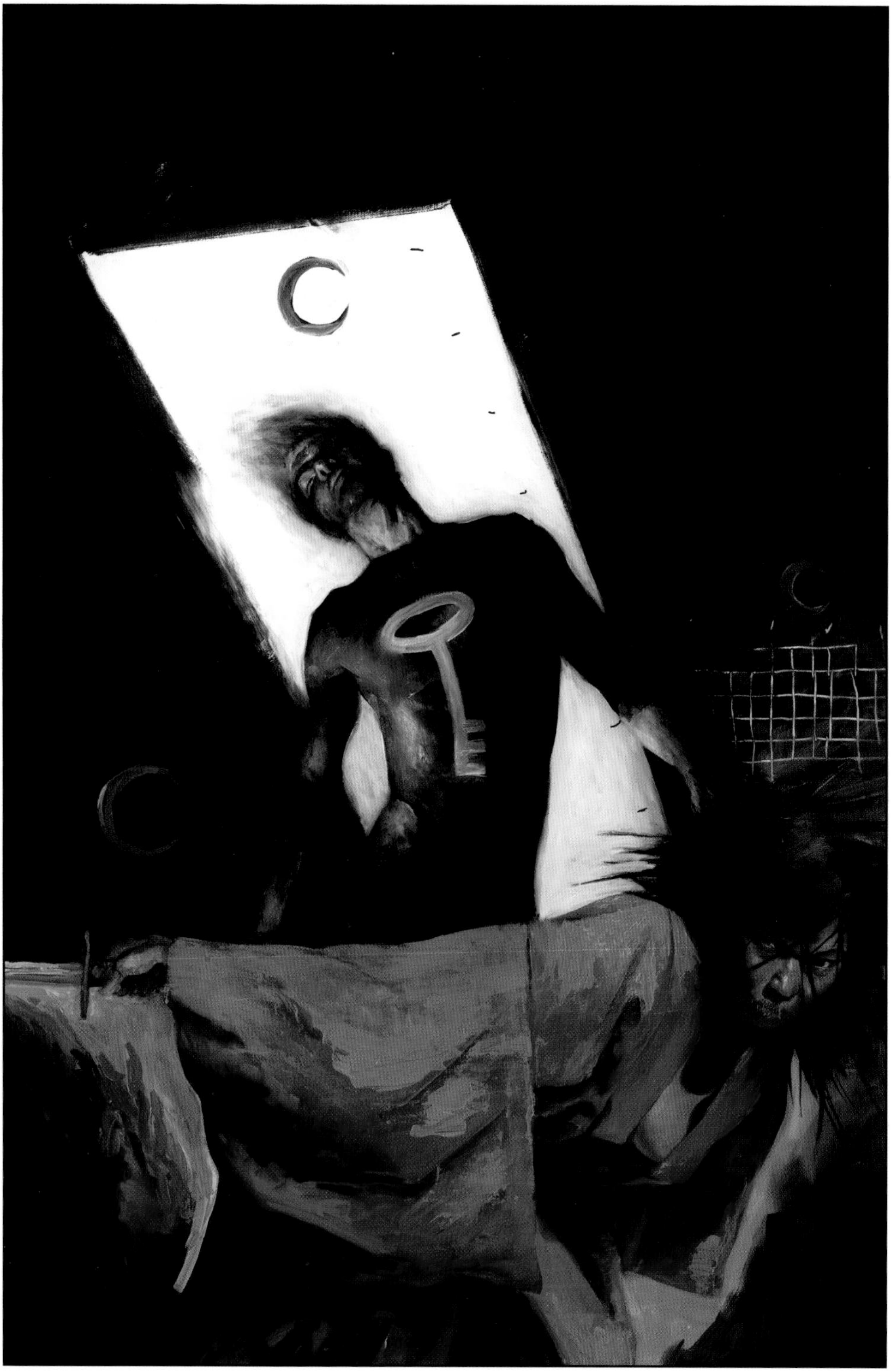

JASON SHAWN ALEXANDER

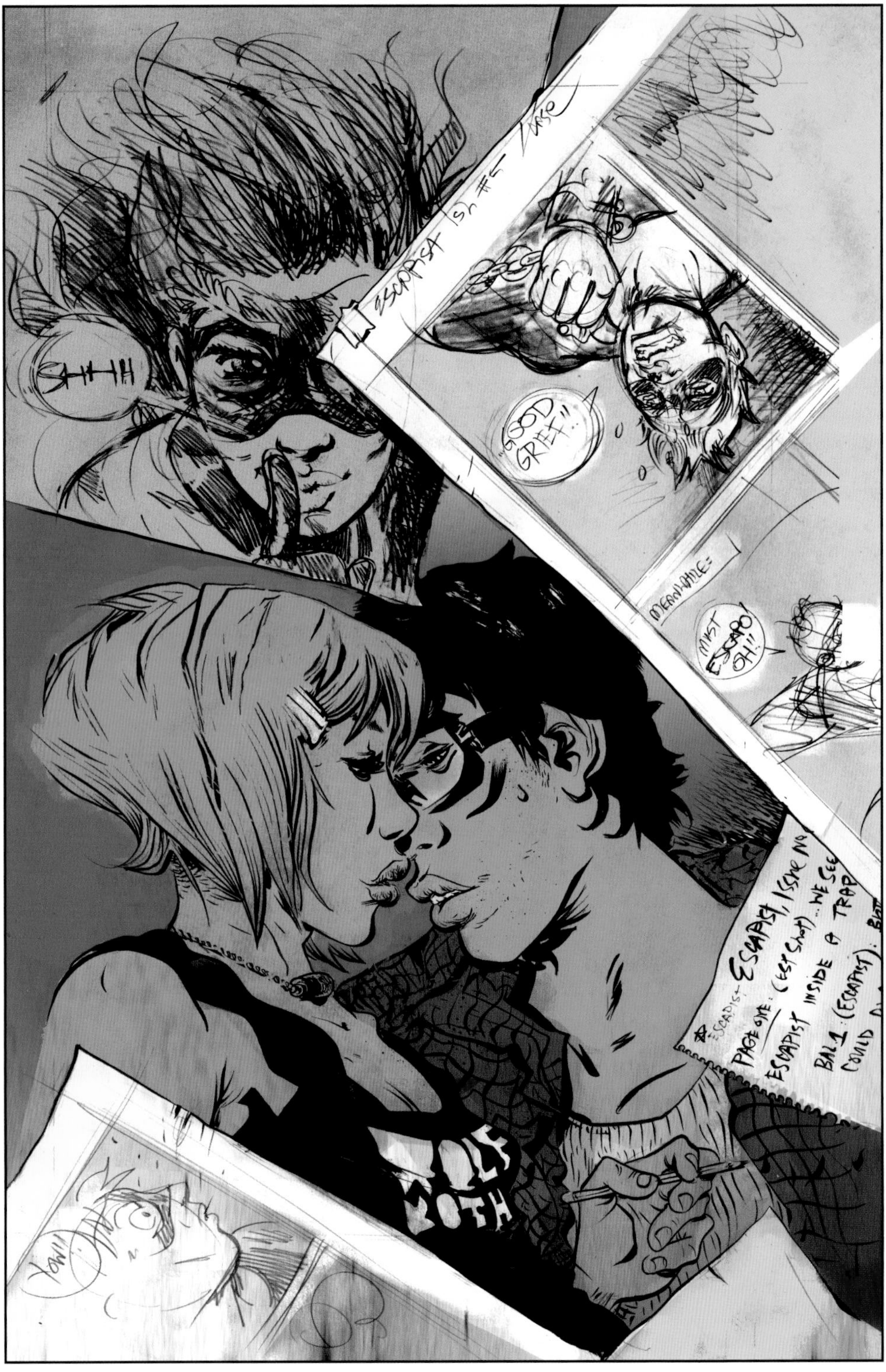
SHHHH
GOOD GRIEF!!
MEANWHILE:
MUST ESCAPO OH!!
YOW!!
ESCAPIST, Issue No
PAGE ONE: (EST Shot)... WE SEE ESCAPIST INSIDE A TRAP
BAL 1: (ESCAPIST):
COULD

PAUL POPE

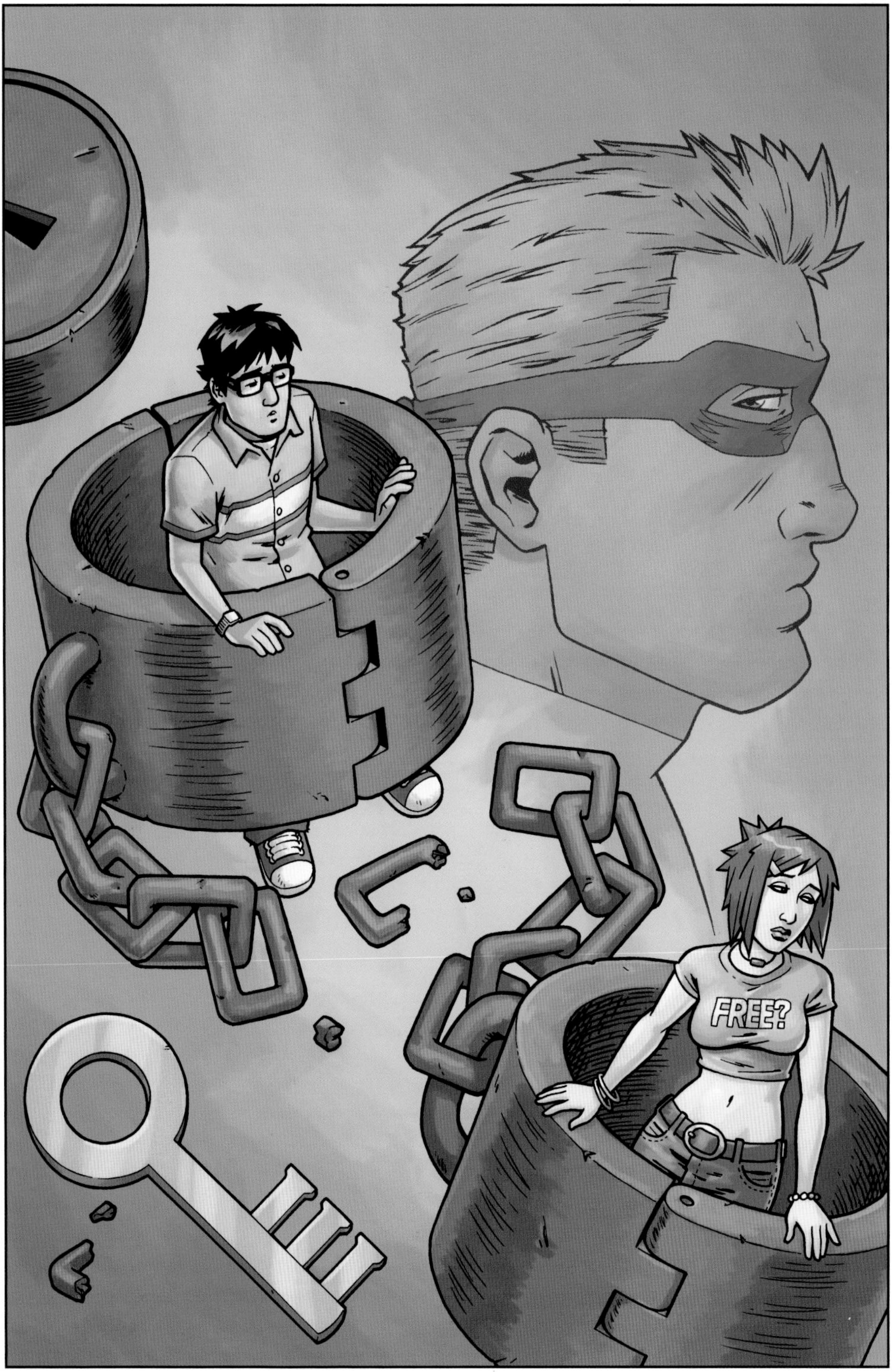
FREE?

STEVE ROLSTON • Color by Dave Stewart

ESCAPIST COVER GALLERY

○━ω

T HE FOLLOWING PAGES feature the three "faux" comics covers specially designed and used in the context of *The Escapists* story line.

JASON SHAWN ALEXANDER • Color by Matthew Hollingsworth

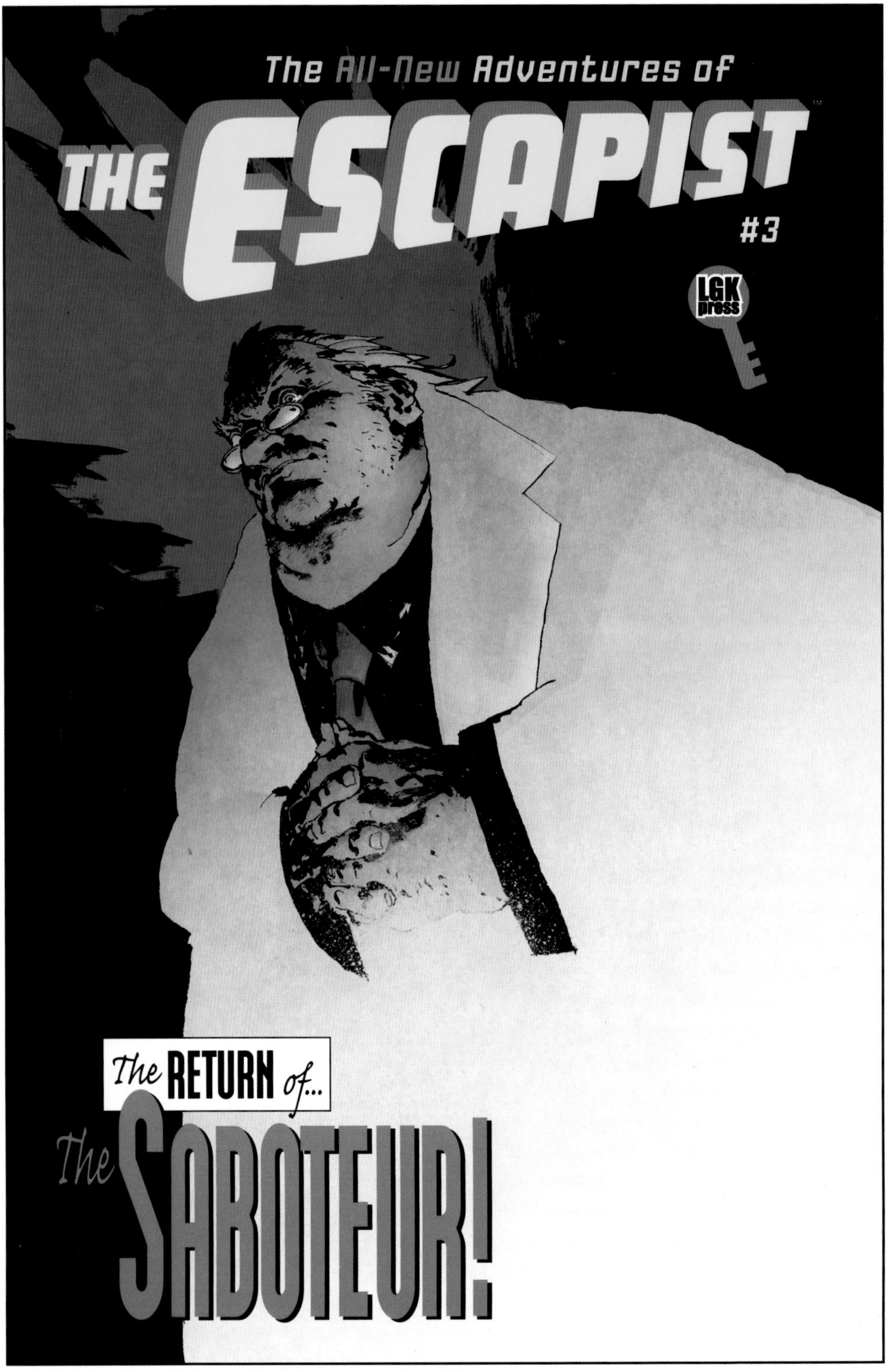
The All-New Adventures of
THE ESCAPIST
#3
LGK press
The RETURN of...
The SABOTEUR!

JASON SHAWN ALEXANDER • Color by Matthew Hollingsworth

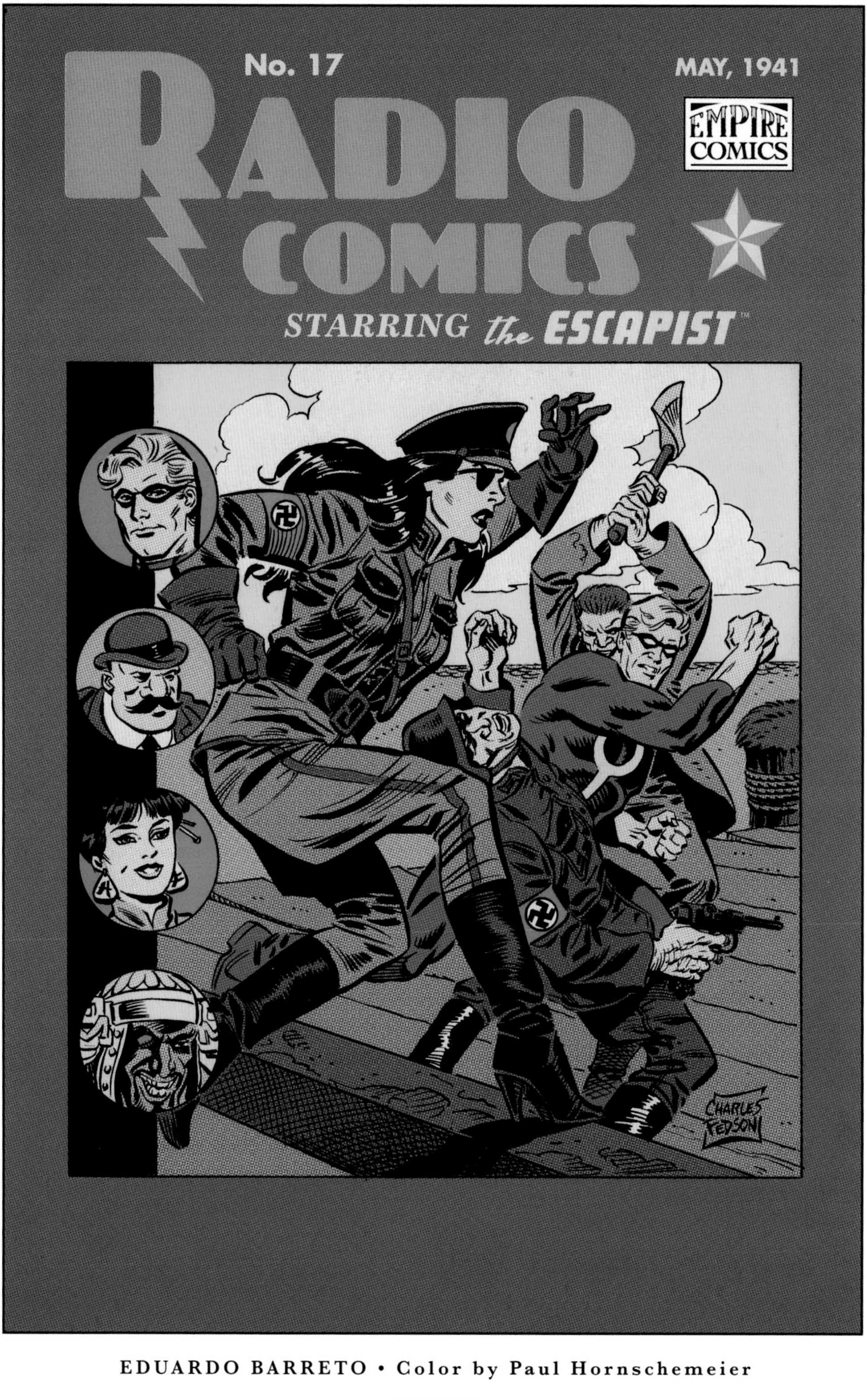
No. 17
MAY, 1941
RADIO COMICS
EMPIRE COMICS
STARRING the ESCAPIST™
CHARLES FEDSON

EDUARDO BARRETO • Color by Paul Hornschemeier

CREATOR BIOGRAPHIES

JASON SHAWN ALEXANDER's art is primarily rooted in illustration and comics work, though his personal paintings are gathering gallery attention. Besides Dark Horse, he's worked for Image, DC, and Oni Press, where he received two Eisner Award nominations for his run on *Queen & Country*. In addition, Jason was awarded a silver medal from the Society of Illustrators West for his cover work on *Damn Nation* for Dark Horse. He lives in Los Angeles.

Uruguayan EDUARDO BARRETO enjoys international notoriety as the artist behind such high-profile titles as *Batman, Superman, Star Wars, Green Arrow, Daredevil,* and *Aliens/Predator*. Over the course of his career he has worked for DC, Marvel, Archie Comics, Western Publishing, Dark Horse, Oni Press, and a variety of newspaper and advertising companies. He is also the artist of the long-running *Judge Parker* newspaper strip for King Features. *Photo by Diana Schutz.*

Eisner, Harvey, and Inkpot Award-winning artist BRIAN BOLLAND began his comics career in a variety of underground U.K. magazines. His first regular work was *Powerman*, with Dave Gibbons, which was distributed in Nigeria from 1975 to 1977. Bolland is perhaps best known for his work on *The Killing Joke* with Alan Moore and on *Judge Dredd*, as well as for his covers to such titles as *The Invisibles, Animal Man, Wonder Woman, Batman,* and *Tank Girl*. His latest collections are *Bolland Strips!* from Knockabout and *The Art of Brian Bolland* from Image.

PHILIP BOND first gained a fan following through his creation *Wired World*, which began with the first issue of *Deadline*, the landmark U.K. comics magazine. He has since gone on to draw *Tank Girl; Kill Your Boyfriend; The Invisibles; Hellblazer: Bad Blood;* and *Vertigo Pop: London*, among others. In addition to cover art for *The Exterminators*, his recent work for Vertigo/DC includes the miniseries *Vimanarama*, a co-creation with Grant Morrison. Bond lives in New Jersey with his family.

In addition to his comics art, multiple Eisner Award winner JOHN CASSADAY has also designed works for Ringling Bros. and Barnum & Bailey Circus, Levi's Blue Jeans, and German hip-hop band Die Firma. His art has been exhibited in Hong Kong, New York City, and the Smithsonian Institute in Washington, DC. John lives in New York City and is currently working on *Astonishing X-Men* with Joss Whedon.

MATT HOLLINGSWORTH is great at brewing his own beer, but he makes a living as one of the most prolific and talented colorists working in comics today. He attended the Joe Kubert School of Cartoon Art before moving on to color such books as *Preacher, Hellboy, Catwoman, Grendel Tales: Devils and Deaths, The Eternals,* and *Daredevil.* He is currently living in Croatia.

The Ignatz, Eisner, and Harvey Award-nominated cartoonist PAUL HORNSCHEMEIER lives in Chicago. His groundbreaking serial *Sequential* is collected in a hardcover of the same name, and his other critically acclaimed series, *Forlorn Funnies,* is collected in the poignant *Mother, Come Home* from Dark Horse Books and in *Let Us Be Perfectly Clear* from Fantagraphics Books. His most recent work, *The Three Paradoxes*, is published by Fantagraphics.

DAN JACKSON has worked as an in-house digital production specialist at Dark Horse for over ten years. In addition, he has lent his coloring talents to a variety of titles, including *Star Wars* and *The Amazing Adventures of the Escapist,* among many others. He lives in Portland, Oregon, with his wife and two daughters.

JAMES JEAN is an award-winning illustrator living in Los Angeles. He was born in Taiwan in 1979, raised in New Jersey, and educated at the School of Visual Arts in New York City. Upon graduating in 2001, he quickly became an acclaimed cover artist for DC Comics, garnering four consecutive Eisner awards, two Harvey awards, and a gold medal from the Society of Illustrators of L.A. He has also contributed to many national and international publications. His clients include *Time Magazine, The New York Times, Rolling Stone, Spin, ESPN, Atlantic Records, Target, Playboy,* and *Knopf,* among others.

FRANK MILLER currently writes *All Star Batman and Robin the Boy Wonder*, but he began his comics career in the '70s, revitalizing Marvel's *Daredevil*. He then took his talents to DC, where he reinvented Batman in 1986 with *Batman: The Dark Knight Returns*. Its sequel, *Batman: The Dark Knight Strikes Again*, published fifteen years later, broke all industry sales records. Prior to that, Miller developed a host of creator-owned projects: *The Big Guy and Rusty the Boy Robot* with Geof Darrow, *Martha Washington* with Dave Gibbons, *Bad Boy* with Simon Bisley, and the multiple award-winning *300* with Lynn Varley, now a major motion picture. Miller's popular *Sin City* series has garnered many Eisner and Harvey Awards, and spawned a successful film, co-directed by Miller and Robert Rodriguez. *Photo by Diana Schutz.*

TOM ORZECHOWSKI has been associated with most of the publishers around. He lettered Marvel's *Uncanny X-Men* from the beginning, and stayed with it for eighteen years. At the same time (mid-'70s) he worked in the final true undergrounds. Since 1989, he's lettered manga for Viz, Eclipse, and Dark Horse, specializing in Masamune Shirow's books. His current work includes *Spawn, New Excalibur,* and *Ghost in the Shell 1.5*. *Photo by Lois Buhalis.*

PAUL POPE is the visionary cartoonist behind such titles as *THB, The One Trick Rip-Off,* and *Batman Year 100*. Having begun his career as a self-publisher, in 1995 he became the first Western artist to be signed to a five-year contract with Kodansha, Japan's largest manga publisher. Since then, his works have included *Heavy Liquid* and *100%* at DC/Vertigo, as well as "Teenage Sidekick," a story in DC's *Solo* which garnered him his first Eisner Award, and the Eisner Award-winning *Batman: Year 100*. He lives and works in New York City. *Photo by Aliya Naumoff.*

STEVE ROLSTON is best known as the premier artist on the Eisner Award-winning espionage series *Queen & Country*. His other illustration credits include *Pounded, Jingle Belle,* and *MEK*. With both his artist and writer hats on, he created the cartoony *Jack Spade & Tony Two-Fist* and the "slacker noir" graphic novel *One Bad Day*. Steve lives in Vancouver, Canada, and can be digitally located at <www.steverolston.com>.

 ALEX ROSS revolutionized painting in comics with *Marvels* at Marvel in 1993, *Kingdom Come* at DC in 1996, and *Uncle Sam* at Vertigo in 1998. Between 1998 and 2003, Ross brought Superman, Batman, Captain Marvel, and Wonder Woman to life in a series of tabloid-sized comics celebrating the sixtieth anniversaries of these icons. Ross worked as character designer and co-plotter for the *Earth X, Universe X,* and *Paradise X* trilogy for Marvel, and co-plotted and painted the series *Justice* for DC. Ross also painted the poster for the 2002 Academy Awards, the opening credits for *Spider-Man 2*, and multiple album and DVD covers.

 DAVE STEWART started out as a design intern at Dark Horse, and is now the award-winning colorist of *Hellboy, Superman, Batman,* and many, many other books. In addition to coloring some of the best artists in comics, he practices kung fu, speaks Cherokee, and raises Chihuahuas, which makes him a cross-cultural triple threat in his native state of Idaho.

 Multiple Eisner Award-winning writer BRIAN K. VAUGHAN is best known for penning the runaway hit *Y–The Last Man.* Co-creating such titles as *Runaways, Ex Machina,* and the graphic novel *Pride of Baghdad*, Vaughan has also grappled with such characters as Batman, Spider-Man, and the X-Men. A former magician and president of his high school's "Circus Club," Brian used to perform a straitjacket routine that would make the Escapist cringe.

 MICHAEL CHABON is an amazing writer and an equally amazing person, according to his editor.

EDITOR
DIANA SCHUTZ

ASSISTANT EDITOR
DAVE MARSHALL

BOOK DESIGN
AMY ARENDTS
TINA ALESSI

LOGO DESIGN
LIA RIBACCHI

DIGITAL PRODUCTION
DAN JACKSON
RICH POWERS

PUBLISHER
MIKE RICHARDSON

THE ESCAPISTS™

This volume collects issues one through six of the Dark Horse comic book series *The Escapists*.

Published by Dark Horse Books
A division of Dark Horse Comics, Inc.
10956 SE Main Street
Milwaukie, Oregon 97222
United States of America

www.darkhorse.com
www.MichaelChabon.com

Representation for Michael Chabon
by Mary Evans, Inc. Literary Agency
and Law Offices of Harris M. Miller II, P.C.

First Edition: December 2007
ISBN: 978-1-59307-831-7

10 9 8 7 6 5 4 3 2 1

PRINTED IN CHINA